Rolf Hasse und Uwe Vollmer (Hg.)

Incentives and Economic Behaviour

Schriften
zu Ordnungsfragen der Wirtschaft

Herausgegeben von

Prof. Dr. Gernot Gutmann, Köln
Dr. Hannelore Hamel, Marburg
Prof. Dr. Helmut Leipold, Marburg
Prof. Dr. Alfred Schüller, Marburg
Prof. Dr. H. Jörg Thieme, Düsseldorf

Unter Mitwirkung von

Prof. Dr. Dieter Cassel, Duisburg
Prof. Dr. Karl-Hans Hartwig, Münster
Prof. Dr. Hans-Günter Krüsselberg, Marburg
Prof. Dr. Ulrich Wagner, Pforzheim

Redaktion: Dr. Hannelore Hamel

Band 76: Incentives and Economic Behaviour

 Lucius & Lucius · Stuttgart · 2005

Incentives and Economic Behaviour

Herausgegeben von

Rolf Hasse und **Uwe Vollmer**

Mit Beiträgen von

Diemo Dietrich, Winand Emons, Torsten Eymann,
Silvia Föhr, Dalia Marin, Arnold Picot, Harald Wiese

 Lucius & Lucius · Stuttgart · 2005

Anschriften der Herausgeber:

Prof. Dr. Rolf Hasse
Universität Leipzig
Wirtschaftswissenschaftliche Fakultät
Marschnerstraße 31
04109 Leipzig

Prof. Dr. Uwe Vollmer
Universität Leipzig
Wirtschaftswissenschaftliche Fakultät
Marschnerstraße 31
04109 Leipzig

Bibliografische Information der Deutschen Bibliothek

Die Deutsche Bibliothek verzeichnet diese Publikation in der Deutschen
Nationalbibliografie; detaillierte bibliografische Daten sind im Internet über
http://dnb.ddb.de abrufbar.

© Lucius & Lucius Verlags-GmbH • Stuttgart • 2005
Gerokstraße 51 • D-70184 Stuttgart

Druck und Einband: ROSCH-BUCH Druckerei GmbH, 96110 Scheßlitz
Printed in Germany

ISBN 3-8282-0308-6
ISSN 1432-9220

Vorwort

Der Band enthält die schriftliche Fassung von Beiträgen, die im Herbst 2003 anlässlich des 10-jährigen Jubiläums der Wiedergründung der Wirtschaftswissenschaftlichen Fakultät auf einem wissenschaftlichen Kolloquium in Leipzig vorgestellt wurden. Darüber hinaus wurden zwei weitere Beiträge aufgenommen. Anliegen des Kolloquiums war, den Zusammenhang zwischen Anreizen und ökonomischer Effizienz am Beispiel ausgewählter Themenbereiche zu diskutieren und dabei auch eine Brücke zu Nachbardisziplinen der Wirtschaftswissenschaft zu schlagen.

Der erste Beitrag von *Arnold Picot* mit dem Titel „Der Beitrag der Institutionenökonomik zur Entwicklung der Wirtschaftswissenschaften" beinhaltet den Festvortrag und gibt einen Überblick über bisherige Ergebnisse der Institutionenökonomik und einen Ausblick auf neue Forschungsgebiete. Die nachfolgenden Beiträge haben spezielle Aspekte zum Zusammenhang zwischen Anreizen und ökonomischer Effizienz zum Gegenstand: Der zweite Beitrag von *Winand Emons* mit dem Titel „Credence Goods: The Monopoly Case" beschäftigt sich mit der Bereitstellung von „Vertrauensgütern". Dabei handelt es sich um Güter, deren Anbieter nicht nur die Produktionsleistung erbringen, sondern auch über Expertenwissen verfügen, in welchem Umfang und in welcher Qualität der Nachfrager das Gut benötigt. Da der Konsument die Wahrhaftigkeit dieser Expertise nicht beurteilen kann, bestehen Anreize für den Anbieter, sich opportunistisch zu verhalten. Der Aufsatz behandelt den Fall, in dem der Anbieter als Monopolist auftritt und zeigt, dass selbst in dieser Situation ein Gleichgewicht mit effizienter Allokation zustande kommen kann, bei dem sich alle Anbieter ehrlich verhalten, sofern die Produktionskapazität des Anbieters bekannt ist.

Erkenntnisleitend für den dritten Beitrag von *Dalia Marin* mit dem Titel „Law in Transition and Development: The Case of Russia" ist die Beobachtung, dass in einigen ehemaligen GUS-Mitgliedsstaaten, wie der Ukraine oder Russland, Barterhandel zwischen den Unternehmen sowie zwischenbetriebliche Verschuldung von großer Bedeutung sind. Die Arbeit betrachtet als Ursache für das Entstehen des Barterhandels ein unzulängliches Rechtssystem, das es Gläubigern erschwert, ihre Ansprüche gegenüber Schuldnern geltend zu machen. Damit ein Liefervertrag trotzdem zustande kommt, bietet der Schuldner ein Bartergut als Kreditsicherheit an, so dass der Barterhandel eine institutionelle Lösung ist, die trotz mangelnder Rechtssicherheit den Abschluss lohnender Transaktionen ermöglicht. Die Brücke zur Wirtschaftsinformatik bildete der vierte Beitrag von *Torsten Eymann* mit dem Titel „Rational (Software-) Agents". Software Agents sind selbständig agierende Computerprogramme (beispielsweise an Wertpapierbörsen), die miteinander in Kontakt treten. Das Referat befasst sich mit der Frage, wie Software Agents rationalerweise ausgestaltet sein sollten, damit sie die ihnen von ihrem menschlichen Prinzipal vorgegebenen Ziele bestmöglich realisieren.

Ausgangspunkt des Beitrags von *Diemo Dietrich* mit dem Titel „Monetary Policy and Bank Lending in Japan: An Agency-based Approach" ist die Beobachtung, dass expansive geldpolitische Impulse bei niedrigen Marktzinssätzen mit einem Rückgang des Bankkreditvolumens verbunden sein können, wofür die japanische Episode Ende der 90er Jahre beispielhaft ist. Das Papier erklärt dies im Rahmen eines Prinzipal-Agenten-Modells der Unternehmensfinanzierung, das die Anreize für Geschäftsbanken berücksichtigt, Kreditnehmer zu überwachen. Im letzten Beitrag mit dem Titel „Intrinsische Motivation und Delegation" untersuchen *Silvia Föhr* und *Harald W*iese mithilfe der Prinzipal-Agenten-Theorie, wie Mitarbeiter zur Verfolgung organisatorischer Ziele zu motivieren sind. Konkret geht es dabei um die Monotoniethese: Veranlasst eine verstärkte Kontrolle des Agenten durch den Prinzipal und/oder eine höhere Belohnung für ein Verhalten im Interesse des Prinzipals den Agenten tatsächlich zu zielkonformem Verhalten? Den formalen Analyserahmen für diese Frage liefert ein Modell zur Delegation, das die Autoren geeignet erweitern, um die Gefahr aufzuzeigen, dass intrinsische Motivation durch die Intervention des Prinzipals verdrängt wird.

Dieser Band ist natürlich nicht ohne die Hilfe Anderer entstanden, denen wir herzlich danken. Dieser Dank gebührt in erster Linie den Referenten, die durch ihr Erscheinen zum Gelingen der Veranstaltung beigetragen haben, sowie Frau *Christine Ös* und Frau *Cathérine Lampe*, die die Veranstaltung organisatorisch betreut haben. Frau *Martina Kussatz* und *Matthias Folk* haben das Manuskript in eine druckreife Form gebracht. Besonders danken möchten wir der *Fritz-Thyssen-Stiftung*, deren großzügige finanzielle Unterstützung die Veranstaltung erst hat möglich werden lassen.

Leipzig, im Dezember 2004   *Rolf Hasse* und *Uwe Vollmer*

Inhalt

I. Festvortrag

II. Wissenschaftliches Kolloquium

I.
Festvortrag

Rolf Hasse und Uwe Vollmer (eds.)
Incentives and Economic Behaviour
Schriften zu Ordnungsfragen der Wirtschaft · Band 76 · Stuttgart · 2005

Der Beitrag der Institutionenökonomik zur Entwicklung der Wirtschaftswissenschaften

Arnold Picot

Festveranstaltung

10 Jahre Neugründung der Fakultät für Wirtschaftswissenschaften der Universität

Leipzig

13. November 2003

Es ist mir eine große Freude und Ehre zugleich, heute aus diesem schönen Anlass bei Ihnen zu Gast sein und bei dieser Festveranstaltung einen Vortrag halten zu dürfen.

Leipzig fühle ich mich in mancher Hinsicht verbunden: Mein Großvater war hier in der Zeit nach dem ersten Weltkrieg bis in die dreißiger Jahre hinein Reichgerichtsrat, so dass mein Vater in Leipzig einen großen Teil seiner Jugend und frühen Berufstätigkeit verbrachte. Daher lernte ich auch schon früh von ihm, welchen Unterschied die Sachsen zwischen Leipzig und Dresden sehen: „Die Dresdener können sich dräsden, aber die Leipziger können sich nicht leipzigern!" Nun, dafür können sie vielleicht manches anderes!

Gleich nach der Wende besuchte ich auf Einladung von Leipziger Kollegen diese Universität, war beeindruckt von dem Elan, mit dem sogleich vieles hier in Angriff genommen wurde, aber auch betroffen etwa davon, den Ort der weggesprengten Universitätskirche oder das nahezu in sich zusammenbrechende ehemalige Haus meiner Großeltern in der Gustav-Adolf-Straße zu sehen. Morgens früh joggte ich durch die schönen Leipziger Parks in der seinerzeit noch typisch braunkohlengeschwängerten Luft, besuchte die großen Leipziger Sehenswürdigkeiten und erhielt auch eine informelle Anfrage, in der Gründungskommission dieser Fakultät mitzuwirken. Da ich gleichzeitig schon offiziell gefragt worden war, bei der Neugründung der wirtschafts-wissenschaftlichen Fakultät der Bergakademie Freiberg zu helfen, führte mich meine Aktivität in Sachsen dann allerdings vermehrt an den Rand des Erzgebirges.

Natürlich war ich verschiedentlich während der vergangenen 13 Jahre in dieser immer schöner werdenden Stadt, u.a. auch bei den Feierlichkeiten aus Anlass des 100-jährigen Bestehens der benachbarten Handelshochschule.

Herzlichen Dank also für die heutige Einladung, die ich gern angenommen habe! Diesen Dank verbinde ich mit meinem aufrichtigen Glückwunsch zu dem schönen Jubiläumsanlass sowie mit meiner Gratulation und Anerkennung für das Erreichte, insbesondere für die offene und moderne Ausrichtung dieser Fakultät.

Im Mittelpunkt des mir gestellten Themas steht die Institutionenökonomik – ein Kunstbegriff, den es vorab zu erläutern gilt, ehe wir uns der Frage zuwenden können, warum und in welcher Weise diese Denkrichtung die Wirtschaftwissenschaften – BWL wie VWL – beeinflusst und verändert habe. Der Begriff der IÖ zerfällt in die beiden Komponenten *Institution* und *Ökonomik*.

Beginnen wir mit dem auf den ersten Blick einfacheren, der *Ökonomik*. Ökonomik ist die Wissenschaft von der Ökonomie, also von der Wirtschaft, der Einzel- oder Gesamtwirtschaft. Dabei geht es bei der Ökonomik darum, die Handlungen von Menschen unter Knappheitsbedingungen zu erklären und zu gestalten. Die Ökonomik unterstellt ein selbstinteressiertes Individuum, das gemäß seinen individuellen Präferenzen unter Beachtung der jeweils gegebenen finanziellen, zeitlichen oder wissensbezogenen Restriktionen in möglichst rationaler, Vor- und Nachteile abwägender Weise Entscheidungen auswählt. Der Aspekt des eigeninteressierten Handelns beinhaltet dabei die Möglichkeit sehr unterschiedlicher individueller Zielvorstellungen – altruistischer oder egoistischer –, und er schließt ein, dass damit gerechnet werden muss, dass ein Akteur seine Ziele ggf. auch unter Inkaufnahme der Verletzung von Präferenzen anderer Individuen bzw. von herrschenden Normen verfolgt, wenn er sich davon einen Vorteil verspricht (so genannter Opportunismus). Die Ökonomik interessiert sich – im Unterschied zur Psychologie – nicht für das einzelne Individuum und dessen ganz spezifische Eigenarten, sondern für die *typischen* Verhaltensweisen, die der Tendenz nach häufiger anzutreffen sind. Sie geht zudem vom Prinzip des so genannten methodologischen Individualismus aus, welches besagt, dass alle Eigenschaften eines sozialen Systems letztlich von den Handlungsweisen und Anreizbedingungen der Individuen abhängen und dass diese mit ihren Verhaltensweisen und Entscheidungen das soziale System und seine Ordnung konstituieren. Dieses Verständnis von Ökonomik und das damit verbundene realistische Menschenbild liegen auch der Institutionenökonomik zu Grunde.

Was hat es aber nun mit den *Institutionen* auf sich? Wer sich unvoreingenommen etwa als Laie dem Begriff „Wirtschaft" zuwendet, wird vermutlich als erstes auf den Gedanken kommen, dass es dort um Geld, um Märkte, um Nachfrage und deren Befriedigung, um den sinnvollen Einsatz knapper Produktionsfaktoren, um Beschäftigung und Wohlstand oder Ähnliches geht, aber Institutionen?

Der Institutionenbegriff ist von vorneherein nicht einfach. Er wird oftmals eher dem Bereich der Soziologie, der Politologie und der Rechtswissenschaft zugeordnet als der Wissenschaft von der Wirtschaft. Wer erinnert sich nicht an den „Marsch durch die Institutionen", den die 68er angeblich antreten wollten?

Schaut man in die verschiedenen gesellschaftswissenschaftlichen Disziplinen, die sich des Institutionenbegriffs bedienen, so stößt man auf eine kaum überbietbare Vielfalt von Begriffsverständnissen, wird das Wort „doch auf so unterschiedliche Phänomene, wie z.B. den Industriebetrieb, die Ehe, den Staat, die Gastfreundschaft oder das Kindergeld, angewandt." (*Dietl* 1993, S. 35). Die 20 Uhr-Nachrichten der Tagesschau, das Grundgesetz oder der Handschlag zwischen Kaufleuten lassen sich ebenso als Institutionen bezeichnen wie der wöchentliche Stammtisch, die Kommunalverwaltung, das Geld, die Sprache, die Fußballbundesliga oder die Marke *Coca-Cola*. Auf den ersten Blick lässt sich also jede irgendwie dauerhafte, der menschlichen Kultur zuzurechnende Einrichtung als Institution verstehen – gleichgültig ob es sich um organisierte Gebilde (Unternehmen, Verwaltungen) oder um förmliche Normen (Grundgesetz und Spezialgesetze), um evolutorisch gewachsene (Sprache, Handschlag zwischen Kaufleuten) oder bewusst gestaltete Erscheinungen (formulierter Vertrag, organisatorische Regeln) handelt.

Das damit angesprochene Merkmal der *Dauerhaftigkeit* allein ist aber nicht zureichend, um Institutionen von sonstigen Gebilden abzugrenzen. Denn wir würden eine im Museum zur Schau gestellte alte Maschine, ein altes Foto oder ein Jahrhunderte altes

Gebäude zwar zur menschlichen Kultur zählen, aber nicht ohne weiteres als Institution bezeichnen. Es muss vielmehr etwas zu der relativen Dauerhaftigkeit hinzutreten, damit von einer Institution die Rede sein kann. Dieses Etwas sind *Erwartungen*. Man knüpft an eine Institution bestimmte Erwartungen: Vom Handschlag der Kaufleute erwartet man, dass das damit besiegelte Wort beiderseitig honoriert wird, von der Marke *Coca-Cola* eine bestimmte Produktqualität und ein gewisses Konsumerleben, von dem Industriebetrieb in Form einer AG bestimmte Verhaltensweisen auf Kapital- und Gütermärkten, von den auf der Grundlage des Grundgesetzes erlassenen Gesetzesnormen Orientierung und Hilfestellung für ein funktionierendes Gemeinwesen, vom Geld, dass es als Tauschmittel akzeptiert wird, von der Sprache, dass sie in bestimmten Kontexten verstanden wird usw. Eine Institution wäre demnach als *Erwartungsbündel* zu verstehen, das sich auf die Verhaltensweisen derjenigen bezieht, die sich dieser Institutionen in irgendeiner Weise bedienen.

Die bisher behandelten Merkmale *Dauerhaftigkeit* und *Verhaltenserwartungen* geben uns bereits einen instruktiven Einblick in das, was Institutionen ausmacht, aber sie allein sind noch nicht hinreichend für das Konzept einer gesellschaftlich bzw. ökonomisch relevanten Institution. Nicht jede regelmäßige Erwartung stellt sich nämlich im sozialen oder wirtschaftlichen Kontext als Institution dar. Die Erwartung eines Konjunkturaufschwungs aufgrund von Monatsberichten der Bundesbank ist etwas anderes als die Erwartung einer Normenbefolgung etwa im Straßenverkehr. Wenn die erste Erwartung enttäuscht wird, so muss man dies einfach hinnehmen, man hat – in aller Regel – keine Möglichkeit, die nicht eingetretene Erwartung doch noch nachträglich durchzusetzen oder zu sanktionieren. Im Falle der Übertretung von Normen aber gibt es ein gesellschaftliches *Sanktionspotenzial*, welches das Abweichen von der Norm unwahrscheinlicher macht.

Dieses Sanktionspotenzial liegt oftmals außerhalb des handelnden Individuums, ist also aus dessen Sicht externer Art: Die förmliche oder auch informelle Aufdeckung und Bestrafung der Erwartungs- bzw. Normverletzung erfolgt durch Dritte; das Abweichen von tradierten gesellschaftlichen Regeln wird vom sozialen Umfeld geächtet (jemand wird geschnitten, weil er sich schlecht benommen, gegen Regeln verstoßen hat), die Übertretung offizieller Normen förmlich bestraft (Zivil- oder Strafverfahren), enttäuschte Markenerwartung durch Abwanderung von Kunden sanktioniert (Marktverhalten). Das Sanktionspotenzial kann auch interner Natur sein (Selbstbindung an Normen aufgrund von Tradition oder Einsicht und das damit verbundene Unwohlfühlen bei Normverletzung). Nicht selten treten externe und interne Sanktionspotenziale gemeinsam auf.

Diese Bemerkungen weisen zugleich darauf hin, dass Institutionen nur dann ihre Wirkung entfalten können, wenn sie von einer größeren Zahl der Akteure des jeweiligen Bezugsbereichs akzeptiert bzw. sogar verinnerlicht werden, wenn die mit ihnen verbundenen Sanktionsmöglichkeiten realistisch und durchsetzbar sind und wenn das Individuum sie als nachteilig empfindet. Wirksame Institutionen setzen also in ihrem jeweiligen Betrachtungsbereich (Unternehmung, Branchen, Gesamtwirtschaft,

Weltwirtschaft) einen gewissen Konsens über ihre Anerkennungswürdigkeit voraus – dass das nicht immer der Fall ist, dafür gibt es viele Beispiele.

Wir können also an dieser Stelle festhalten: Institutionen treten uns in enormer Vielfalt entgegen. Es handelt sich bei ihnen um *kulturell-gesellschaftliche Konstrukte, an die sich bestimmte Verhaltenserwartungen knüpfen und deren Nichteinhaltung sanktionsbewehrt ist*. Weil Institutionen sich in gesellschaftlich-historischen Prozessen herausbilden und in ihrer Wirkung u.a. von der inneren Anerkennung der Beteiligten abhängen, sind sie grundsätzlich dynamische Gebilde und nur mit gewissen Unschärfen erfassbare Gebilde. Das hat selbstverständlich Konsequenzen für ihre Formalisierbarkeit und Abbildbarkeit in quantitativen Modellen.

Wieso könnte nun ein solcher Begriff von Institutionen prägend werden für die Entwicklung der Wirtschaftswissenschaft – gleichgültig ob BWL oder VWL? Die Antwort ist einfach und dennoch noch längst nicht allenthalben im Fach akzeptiert, sie lautet: Weil das Wirtschaftsleben auf allen Ebenen und in allen Bereichen in ganz entscheidendem Ausmaß von Institutionen abhängt. Institutionen setzen sozusagen die Rahmenbedingungen für wirtschaftliches Handeln der Individuen, sie bestimmen damit maßgeblich deren Vor- und Nachteilskalküle, d.h. deren Anreize und Entscheidungsresultate – sei es in Form von kulturell gewachsenen Eigenarten der Kommunikation und Kooperation, sei es in Form gesetzter gesellschaftlicher Ordnung, sei es mit Blick auf spezielles Gesellschafts-, Vertrags-, Steuer-, Arbeits- oder Handelsrecht, sei es in Form organisatorischer Regeln und Systeme bei der Gestaltung von Geschäftsprozessen, Arbeitsplätzen und Führungs- und Anreizsystemen. Warum haben Institutionen diese enorme praktische Bedeutung, warum funktioniert unsere Wirtschaft nicht ohne diese Institutionenvielfalt, also gleichsam reibungslos, mechanisch wie ein Uhrwerk gemäß mathematischen Formeln? Oder andersherum gefragt: Warum hat man nicht immer schon die große Bedeutung von Institutionen in den Mittelpunkt gestellt?

Hierzu müssen wir wiederum ein wenig ausholen.

Einerseits ist die Befassung mit Institutionen in der Wirtschaftswissenschaft so neu nicht. Die historische Schule um die Wende des 19. zum 20. Jahrhundert, die österreichische Schule und die amerikanischen Institutionalisten haben ebenso wie viele betont betriebswirtschaftliche Fachvertreter des vergangenen Jahrhunderts die Vielfalt der wirtschaftlich relevanten Institutionen beschrieben, sie mit den wirtschaftlichen Handlungsweisen verknüpft und bewusst der lange Zeit von der neoklassischen Modellwelt beherrschten ökonomischen Theorie als Alternative gegenüber- bzw. als Ergänzung zur Seite gestellt. Da aber die meisten dieser älteren Ansätze, auf die ich hier leider im Einzelnen nicht eingehen kann, weitgehend im Deskriptiven verharrten und keine Analyse im Sinne von Erklärung (warum gibt es diese Institutionen, warum sind sie entstanden, welche Wirkungen haben sie?) oder Gestaltung (wie lassen sich Institutionen verändern, wie sollten Institutionen zielbezogen gestaltet werden?) anboten, waren sie der Eleganz vieler mathematischer Modellansätze unterlegen, die von derartigen Institutionen abstrahieren. Hinzu kommt, dass die vorwiegend neoklassischen Marktmodelle bzw. technologischen Produktionsmodelle der Mikroökonomie und BWL Mitte des letzten Jahrhunderts, die in idealisierter Weise jeweils vollkommene Rationalität und vollkommene Information bzw. technologische Determiniertheit unterstellten, für bestimmte Fragen sehr leistungsfähig waren (z.B. für die Marktmachtanalyse in statischen Märkten oder bei der Erklärung des technologischen und ökonomischen Zusammenwirkens bestimmter industrieller Produktionsfaktoren) – auf andere Fragen, v.a. Erklärung und Gestaltung von Innovation, Wandel, Marktunvollkommenheiten, Unternehmensstrategien, Organisationsdynamik usw., konnten sie dagegen keine befriedigenden Antworten geben – die institutionell ausgerichteten Fachvertreter jener Zeit freilich auch nicht. Diese relative Unzufriedenheit mit dem wissenschaftlichen Zustand der so genannten älteren Institutionenökonomik verbunden mit der Dominanz und formalen Eleganz der seit Ende des 19. Jahrhunderts stark entwickelten mathematischen Modellökonomik führten zu einem zeitweiligen Verdrängen der Institutionenperspektive aus dem Bewusstsein der vorherrschenden Ökonomik.

Allerdings wuchs auch das Unbehagen an den heroischen Prämissen der Neoklassik einerseits sowie dem Eklektizismus bzw. den starken Vereinfachungen betriebswirtschaftlicher Lehrgebäude andererseits. Insbesondere die Annahme vollkommener Rationalität einschließlich vollständiger Information, die den neoklassischen Modellen und vielen Entscheidungsmodellen zugrunde liegt, erweist sich gerade in einem Ansatz des methodologischen Individualismus, wie die Ökonomik ihn bekanntlich darstellt, als ausgesprochen problematisch. In einer Welt vollkommener Rationalität und Information gibt es nämlich keine wirklichen Entscheidungsprobleme, weil alles ohnehin von vorneherein bekannt und klar ist, Unsicherheit und Komplexität sind durch den allwissenden *homo oeconomicus* ohne weiteres vollkommen zu beherrschen, sind also irrelevant. Folglich stellen sich auch gar nicht die Fragen, an denen sich Entscheidungsträger in der Praxis, ob in Unternehmen, in privaten Haushalten oder in der Politik, die Zähne ausbeißen: Wie kann ich angesichts der Unsicherheit über die künftige Entwicklung meiner Umwelt, unvollkommenen Wissens über die Wirkungen meines Handelns und über die Verhaltensweisen anderer Akteure, mit denen ich kooperiere und konkurriere, sinnvolle Entscheidungen treffen? Welche Systeme und Strukturen können mich dabei wirkungsvoll entlasten und unterstützen? Weder die Neoklassik noch die traditionelle Produktionstheorie kennen derartige Managementprobleme; Strategie oder interne Organisation und Führung von Unternehmen spielen in ihren Aussagensystemen ebenso wenig eine Rolle wie die diversen Instrumente der Information Dritter etwa in Form von Bilanzen oder anderen Kapitalmarktinformationen – alles Fragen, die den einzelwirtschaftlichen Entscheidungsträger wie auch den wirtschaftspolitisch Verantwortlichen brennend interessieren.

Die Aufhebung der Prämisse vollkommenen Wissens, wie sie der IÖ zu Grunde liegt, führt zu realitätsnäheren Aussagensystemen und hat daher ganze Forschergenerationen der modernen Wirtschaftswissenschaft bewegt. *Herbert Simon* war einer der ersten, die etwa Unternehmensorganisationen aus dieser Perspektive heraus konzeptualisierten: „elaborate organizations ... can only be understood as machinery for coping with the limits of man's abilities to comprehend and compute in the face of complexity and uncertainty." (*Simon* 1959, S. 501). Die Informationsökonomik *Stigler*'scher Prägung ist der Versuch einer anderen Antwort auf diese Herausforderung: Über die Anerkennung und Einbeziehung von Suchkosten auf Märkten erscheinen Preisbildung und Marktverhalten in einem ganz anderen Licht. *F.A. von Hayek* hat zu einem sehr frühen Zeitpunkt bereits das Wissensproblem und die Wissensdynamik sowie die Grenzen des „Wissen-Könnens" als eigentlichen Problemkern wirtschaftswissenschaftlicher Fragestellungen erkannt und in den Mittelpunkt seiner Untersuchungen gestellt (vgl. z. B. *Hayek* 1945 oder *Hayek* 1994). Die *Institutionenökonomik*, die mit den vorgenannten Entwicklungen eng verknüpft ist, bietet eine weitere Antwort auf die veränderte Problemsicht. *Douglass North* hat in seinen zahlreichen Werken die zentrale Bedeutung von Institutionen für die wirtschaftliche Entwicklung herausgestellt und dabei die Entstehung, die Wirkungsweise und die Veränderung von Institutionen in einer analytisch-wirtschaftshistorischen Perspektive untersucht (vgl. *North* 1988 oder *North* 1992). *Ronald Coase* hat vermutlich den nicht nur für die BWL bedeutendsten Beitrag geleistet, indem er zum einen mit seiner berühmten *Nature of the Firm* (1937) die Wahl von Institutionen (Hierarchie versus Markt, make or buy) einem theoriegeprägten ökonomischen Kalkül unterworfen und damit die Theorie der Transaktionskosten angestoßen hat. Zum anderen hat er in seinem berühmten *Coase*-Theorem (1960) gezeigt, dass in einer Welt ohne Transaktionskosten institutionelle Regelungen wie Zuordnung und Ausgestaltung von Rechten gleichgültig sind, da ja alle Ansprüche und Konflikte kostenlos ausgehandelt und geregelt werden können, dass aber in einer realen Welt mit Transaktionskosten, in der die Etablierung und Durchsetzung von Normen eben nicht kostenlos ist, institutionelle Arrangements auf das Ergebnis des Wirtschaftsprozesses erheblichen Einfluss nehmen. Mit Hilfe seiner Arbeiten wurde klar: „instiutions matter and are susceptible to analysis" (*Matthews* 1986, S. 903). *Williamson* (1991, S. 7ff.) beschreibt daher die Institutionenökonomik auch treffend als „economizing on bounded rationality". D.h.: Wie kann ich unter den Bedingungen beschränkter Rationalität sinnvoll ökonomisch handeln und wie müssen die Institutionen dafür aufgestellt sein?

Die begrenzte Rationalität der Akteure kann nämlich Schäden verursachen im Sinne falscher Arbeitsteilung, überhöhter Transaktionskosten, entgangener Gewinne. Um derartige Nachteile zu vermindern, entwerfen die Beteiligten Instrumente zur Verbesserung der Rationalität, mit deren Hilfe Koordination und Motivation verbessert, Opportunismus gezügelt und damit Rationalitätslücken verkleinert werden können. Anstatt in jeder wirtschaftlichen Handlungssituation zwischen allen Beteiligten von neuem und mit großem Aufwand alle relevant erscheinenden Aspekte der Zusammenarbeit und des Tausches zu beraten und zu bewerten, stützt man sich auf gegenseitig anerkannte Institutionen. Insofern lassen sich Institutionen als *Rationalitätssurrogate* (*Picot, Dietl* und *Franck* 2002 S. 40) auffassen, also als Ersatzstoffe für Rationalität. Institutionen als durch menschliches Handeln evolutorisch-unabsichtlich zustande gekommene (gemeinsame Kultur, gewachsene Regeln), teils auch als bewusst entworfene und vereinbarte (Organisationssysteme, Verträge) Regelsysteme üben also nur und gerade in einer realen, unsicheren Welt mit unvollkommener Information und Rationalität die enorm wichtige ökonomische Funktion der Rationalisierung arbeitsteiliger Prozesse innerhalb und zwischen Unternehmen sowie auf Märkten aller Art und auch in Staat und Gesellschaft aus. Als sanktionsbewehrte Erwartungsbündel koordinieren sie die Orientierung der beteiligten Individuen, indem man davon ausgehen kann, dass sich alle mit großer Wahrscheinlichkeit daran ausrichten. Sie machen damit zugleich opportunistisches Verhalten unwahrscheinlicher und ermöglichen so, dass der arbeitsteilige wirtschaftliche Prozess mit geringerer Reibung (Transaktionskosten) gelingt. Es findet also ein „economizing on bounded rationality" statt – Institutionen wirken als Rationalitätssurrogate, als Füller von Rationalitätslücken.

Ein Beispiel mag dies erläutern: Wenn im Arbeitsvertrag einer Führungskraft deren Beteiligung am Jahreserfolg des geleiteten Geschäftsbereichs institutionell verankert wird, dann lässt sich dies als Ersatz für die fehlende Beobachtbarkeit ihrer Anstrengungen, Aktivitäten und Absichten durch die beaufsichtigende Ebene interpretieren. Wenn die Aufsichtsebene kostenlos diese Führungskraft vollständig beobachten und beurteilen könnte, dann brauchte sie ein solches Anreizelement nicht, weil die Beobachtung der Vertragserfüllung jederzeit vollkommen möglich wäre. Unter solchen Bedingungen wäre aber auch die Führungskraft überflüssig, weil der Unternehmer mit seinem kostenlosen vollkommenen Wissen den Prozess ohne weiteres direkt und vollständig steuern könnte, ja, es ist sogar fraglich, ob wir überhaupt einen Unternehmer brauchten. Weil das aber nicht so ist, benötigen wir Hilfsmittel, Krücken, die es uns erlauben, trotz der Unvollkommenheiten mit möglichst überschaubarem Aufwand einigermaßen rational kooperieren zu können. Wir sehen hier also ein Beispiel für das *Coase*-Theorem: In einer idealen Welt vollkommener Information spielen Organisation und Vertrag als Steuerungsinstrumente keine Rolle, es ist egal, ob und wie sie ausgestaltet sind. In einer realen Welt, in der die Vereinbarung und Durchsetzung von Zielen nicht trivial, sondern anstrengend und aufwändig sind, benötigen wir Hilfsmittel: Managementstrukturen und Anreizsysteme sind also eine logische Konsequenz der Informationsunvollkommenheit unserer Welt.

Zur möglichst weitgehenden Rationalisierung dieser unvollkommenen Wirtschaftswelt bedarf es zahlreicher Institutionen, deren vergleichsweise Vor- und Nachteilhaftigkeit situationsbezogen zu analysieren ist (komparativer Ansatz) und die durch institutionelle Innovation und institutionellen Wettbewerb ständig weiterzuentwickeln sind. Bilanz- und Publizitätsrecht, Corporate Governance-Regeln, Organisationsdesign, Anreizsysteme sind Beispiele für andauernde institutionelle Analysen und Gestaltungen im Bereich der BWL, die aktuellen politischen Diskussionen um Sozialstaat, Steuersystem, Arbeitspolitik und Föderalismus unterstreichen dieses für den Bereich von VWL, Politik und Staat. Institutionenökonomisches Denken und Handeln und institutionenökonomische Probleme finden sich also auf allen Ebenen von Wirtschaft und Gesellschaft, wo durch bewusste oder unbewusste Herausbildung und Durchsetzung von Normen und Regeln die Koordination, Motivation und Effizienz sozialer

Systeme zu verbessern gesucht wird: In Arbeitsgruppen und Familien, in Unternehmen und zwischenbetrieblichen Netzwerken, in Branchen und Volkswirtschaften sowie in inter- und übernationalen Geflechten. Die IÖ ist daher keiner Einzelwissenschaft, d.h. weder der VWL, noch der BWL, noch der Politologie oder Soziologie allein zuzurechnen, sondern sie stellt ein methodisch-theoretisches Analyseinstrumentarium bereit, das auf sehr unterschiedliche Problemstrukturen und Aggregationsebenen anzuwenden ist. Zugleich eröffnet sie unter einem ökonomischen Blickwinkel enorme Chancen für Interdisziplinarität.

Die Institutionenökonomik bedient sich bei der Bewältigung derartiger Aufgaben diverser theoretisch-methodischer Instrumente, die ich hier nur nennen möchte:

− Die Property Rights-Theorie, die die Zuordnung von Rechten und damit verbunden die Effizienz dieser Zuordnung untersucht,

− die Transaktionskostentheorie, die anhand der Analyse von Kostenstrukturen und ihrer Einflussgrößen Aussagen zum Vergleich und zur Analyse von organisatorischen Lösungen im jeweiligen Ordnungsrahmen trifft, etwa Make-or-Buy Entscheidungen, und die

− Principal-Agent-Theorie sowie die mit ihr eng verbundenen Vertragstheorien, die sich mit den Informationsasymmetrien zwischen Auftraggebern und Auftragnehmern und damit verbundenen Risiken beschäftigt.

Die genannten Konzepte werden heute in praktisch allen Teildisziplinen von VWL und BWL intensiv verwandt − gleichgültig ob im Marketing, in Kapitalmarkt und Finanzierung, in Unternehmensführung, Personal, Organisation und Controlling, ja selbst in der Wirtschaftsinformatik, ferner in der Ordnungs- und Wirtschaftspolitik, in der Wachstums- und Entwicklungstheorie. Sie führen zu einer Wiederannäherung von BWL und VWL im Sinne einer Einheit der Wirtschaftswissenschaft. In nicht wenigen hochangesehenen Fakultäten und Business Schools werden seit einiger Zeit Managementgrundlagen mit institutionenökonomischer Prägung vermittelt.

Methodisch werden die genannten Theorien entweder normativ mit analytisch-modelltheoretischen Ansätzen (also axiomatisch deduktiv) betrieben und/oder positiv, also systematisierend, beschreibend und erklärend auf empirisch-quantitativer oder -qualitativer Basis (empirische Erhebungen, Fallstudien). Immer öfter kommt die Spieltheorie als Analysehilfe zum Einsatz, auch verbunden mit Labor- oder Feldexperimenten.

Der große Ertrag, den diese Forschungen bislang für Wissenschaft und Praxis erbracht haben, ist in einem solchen Festvortrag auch nicht andeutungsweise abzubilden. Bemerkenswert ist, dass in den vergangenen ca. fünf Jahren mindestens sechs deutschsprachige einführende Lehrbücher in BWL und/oder VWL erschienen sind, die sich alle der IÖ als beherrschender theoretischer Grundlage bedienen (*Richter* und *Furubotn* 2003; *Neus* 2003; *Erlei, Leschke* und *Sauerland* 1999; *Homann* und

Suchanek 2004; *Göbel* 2002; *Voigt* 2002), ganz abgesehen von zahlreichen Speziallehr-büchern und Monographien zu Teilgebieten, wie Management und Organisation, Kapitalmarkt und Finanzierung, Personal, Controlling, Marketing, Wirtschaftssysteme, Industrie- und Marktökonomik sowie Tausenden von Fachbeiträgen in wissenschaftlichen Zeitschriften und Sammelwerken weltweit. Wesentliche Zukunftschancen und Verbesserungsmöglichkeiten liegen in der bereits begonnenen, aber noch zu intensivierenden Einbeziehung von Erkenntnissen der angewandten Psychologie bzw. der *behavioral economics* (*Kahnemann, Slovic* und *Tversky* 1982; *Fehr* und *Schmidt* 1999).

So positiv die Gesamtbeurteilung der IÖ für die Entwicklung der Wirtschaftswissenschaft auch ausfällt – es bleiben selbstverständlich offene Fragen und neue Aufgaben. Zum einen ist davor zu warnen, dass das Gebiet dogmatisch erstarrt. Auf internationalen Tagungen hat man zunehmend den Eindruck, dass der wissenschaftliche Nachwuchs technische Fingerübungen meint vorweisen zu müssen, die weniger problemorientiert sind, sondern eher den souveränen Umgang mit schwierigen formalen Modellen (etwa der Prinzipal-Agent-Theorie) unter Beweis stellen. Hier drohen inhaltliche Entleerung und Irrelevanz. Die alte und neue IÖ war getrieben von der Notwendigkeit, bestimmte ökonomische Phänomene besser zu verstehen oder überhaupt erst ökonomisch-theoretisch fassbar zu machen. Das sollte weiterhin das Hauptinteresse sein, nicht die Methodenprahlerei. Und es gibt noch genügend spannende, herausfordernde Fragen, von denen ich abschließend nur eine herausgreifen will.

Ökonomen – gleichgültig ob Betriebs- oder Volkswirte – sind ziemlich gut darin, „bessere" institutionelle Welten zu entwerfen, aber sie tun sich nach wie vor extrem schwer, den Weg vom hier und heute zu diesen Zielen zu weisen bzw. praktisch umzusetzen. Der Prozess des Wandels und der Veränderung von Institutionen ist aber in der Realität mindestens genauso wichtig und erforschungsbedürftig wie der Entwurf alternativer Regelsysteme. Die Interessen- und Pfadabhängigkeit des Verhaltens von Akteuren im Prozess des Wandels, die erforderlichen Anreizmechanismen und die Schwierigkeiten des Wandels großer kollektiver Systeme bedürfen dringend der sorgfältigen, über Berater- und Politikersprüche hinausgehenden institutionenökonomischen Analyse und Gestaltung. Wo liegen jeweils die Grenzen der Veränderbarkeit, wo die Möglichkeiten, welches sind die jeweils begünstigenden Randbedingungen. Dazu kann die IÖ, insbesondere die dynamische Variante (vgl. *Hayek* 1945, 1994 oder *North* 1988, 1992) einiges beitragen, vor allem hinsichtlich Analyse und Beschreibung. Die normative und auch anwendbare Seite hingegen zeigt erst wenige Erkenntnisse (vgl. z.B. *Wolff* 1995; *Picot, Freudenberg* und *Gaßner* 1999, *Picot* und *Fiedler* 2002), auf die ich abschließend nur mit wenigen beispielhaften Hinweisen eingehen möchte (vgl. *Picot* und *Fiedler* 2002):

Wir haben weiter oben gesehen, dass Institutionen teils mehr oder weniger ungewollt gewachsen, teils bewusst geschaffen sind. Was bedeutet das für Reorganisation, Reform oder Restrukturieren, also für die Veränderung von institutionellen Arrangements? Wann kann Wandel durch Fremdorganisation quasi „vorgeschrieben" werden und in welchen Fällen scheinen Evolution und Selbstorganisation der wesentliche Weg zu Veränderung zu sein? Es ist also zu klären, wann sich von selbst neue Institutionen bilden (Selbstentwicklung) und in welchen Fällen Institutionen fremdbestimmt geschaffen werden können bzw. müssen (Fremdorganisation). In diesem Zusammenhang sind unter anderen folgende Einflussgrößen zu berücksichtigen.

Zunächst kommt es darauf an, ob die Betroffenen von einer Institutionenänderung einen positiven *Nettonutzen* erwarten. Eine solche Abschätzung hängt u.a. von den irreversiblen Vorinvestitionen der Beteiligten (sunk costs) und von der Länge ihres Planungs- und Entscheidungshorizonts ab. Veränderungen mit einem klaren positiven Nettonutzen (z.B. Einführung oder Erhöhung von Mindestlöhnen) werden sich eher von selbst durchsetzen als andere, bei denen der Nettonutzen des Einzelnen negativ oder unklar ist bzw. in sehr weiter Ferne liegt (z.B. Verlängerung von Arbeitszeiten). In den letzteren Fällen können geeignete Informationen und Anreize den notwendigen Wandel befördern helfen.

Ferner erscheint es wichtig, ob die Beteiligten im Wandel gleiche *Interessen* verfolgen. Ist dies der Fall, werden sich Institutionen ebenfalls quasi von selbst bilden (z.B. Rechtsfahrgebot), in anderen müssen Kompensationen und Anreize nachhelfen. Die Spieltheorie hat dazu wichtige Einsichten ermöglicht.

Eine weitere Rolle spielt die Art der Institution, die verändert werden soll. So hat sich gezeigt, dass *formgebundene* Institutionen, wie z.B. Gesetze, formale Organisationsregeln oder technische Systeme in vielen Fällen relativ einfach von dritter Seite geändert werden können. Handelt es sich hingegen *nicht um formgebundene* Institutionen, wie z.B. Gebräuche und Sitten, die eher fundamentalen Charakter haben, ist die Veränderung durch Fremdorganisation kaum möglich. Nur Selbstorganisation und Lernen sind bei derartigen Institutionen in der Lage, eine Veränderung herbeizuführen und neue Institutionen zu erschaffen.

Darüber hinaus sprechen *multipolare Machtverteilung* und *verteiltes tazites* Wissen dafür, dass Selbstorganisation sozusagen von unten nach oben unumgänglich ist, eine Einsicht, die gerade für die immer häufiger anzutreffenden wissensbasierten Unternehmen ausgesprochen wichtig ist und Konsequenzen für deren *governance structure* verlangt.

Ein wirksames Management des Wandels muss diese, hier nur beispielhaft angedeuteten Parameter situationsgerecht erkennen und Fremd- mit Selbstorganisationsmaßnahmen in geeigneter Weise kombinieren. Dabei besteht die Kunst darin, die evolutionär-selbstorganisatorischen mit den planerisch-fremdorganisatorischen Elementen so zu verknüpfen, dass die jeweils zugrunde liegende Situation des Wandels zutreffend reflektiert und der intendierte Wandel insgesamt angesteuert wird – eine ausgesprochen schwierige Aufgabe, wie der Befund von über 50 % Fehlschlägen bei tief greifenden Unternehmensreorganisationen zeigt. Die Transformation der ehemaligen Wirtschaftssysteme Mittel- und Osteuropas, aber auch die dringende

Reform und Neuordnung tief in Verhaltensweisen und Bewusstsein verankerter Ordnungssysteme etwa der sozialer Sicherung, der Gesundheit und der Arbeitsmärkte oder die verspäteten bzw. erfolglosen Strategie- und Organisationsanpassungen vieler Unternehmen sind beredte Beispiele dafür, dass es beim Management des Wandels von Institutionen nicht selten zu naiven Fehleinschätzungen hinsichtlich des Charakters und der Veränderbarkeit von institutionellen Verhältnissen kommt. Selbst bei existenzieller Bedrohung fällt es schwer, den Wandel von Institutionen rechtzeitig, umfassend und nachhaltig zu bewerkstelligen.

Dieses Forschungsfeld der ökonomisch fundierten Beförderung und Begleitung des Wandels von Institutionen und Regelsystemen steckt noch in den Kinderschuhen, auch wenn Gebiete wie Public Choice, Systemtheorie, Organisations- und Verhaltenswissenschaft und nicht zuletzt die Institutionenökonomik selbst dazu beigetragen haben. Dabei handelt es sich um ein zutiefst ökonomisches Problem: zeitlich, sachlich und interessenbezogen interdependente Wahlhandlungen unter Knappheitsbedingungen (Zeit, Budget) bei z.T. erheblichen sunk costs und Pfadabhängigkeiten aller Beteiligten. Mögen sich künftige Forschergenerationen mit den Fragen der Steuerung des institutionellen Wandels intensiver befassen als die vorigen – angesichts der zahlreichen einzel-, gesamt- und weltwirtschaftlichen Herausforderungen benötigen wir die Fähigkeit zur Veränderung vieler – nicht aller! – Institutionen auf allen Ebenen: in Unternehmen, Branchen, Volks- und Weltwirtschaft!

Literatur

Coase, R. H. (1937), The Nature of the Firm, in: Economica, Vol. 4, No. 16, S. 386-405.

Coase, R. H. (1960), The Problem of Social Cost, in: Journal of Law and Economics, Vol. 3, No. 1, S. 1-44.

Dietl, H. (1993), Institutionen und Zeit, Tübingen.

Erlei, M.; M. Leschke und *D. Sauerland* (1999), Neue Institutionenökonomik, Stuttgart.

Fehr, E. und *K. Schmidt* (1999), A Theory of Fairness, Competition, and Cooperation, in: The Quarterly Journal of Economics, Vol. 114, S. 817-868.

Göbel, E. (2002), Neue Institutionenökonomik – Konzeption und betriebswirtschaftliche Anwendungen, Stuttgart.

Hayek, F. A. von (1945), The Use of Knowledge in Society, in: American Economic Review, Vol. 35, No. 4, S. 519-530.

Hayek, F. A. von (1994), Der Wettbewerb als Entdeckungsverfahren, in: *Hayek, F. A. von* (Hrsg.), Freiburger Studien: Gesammelte Aufsätze von Hayek, F. a. v., 2. Aufl., Tübingen.

Homann, K. und *A. Suchanek* (2004), Ökonomik. Eine Einführung, 2. Aufl., Tübingen.

Kahnemann, D.; P. Slovic und *A. Tversky* (1982), Judgment under Uncertainty Heuristics and Biases, Cambridge, MA.

Matthews, R. C. O. (1986), The Economics of Institutions and the Sources of Growth, in: Economic Journal, Vol. 96, No. 4, S. 903-918.

Neus, W. (2003), Einführung in die Betriebswirtschaftslehre aus institutionenökonomischer Sicht, Tübingen.

North, D. C. (1988), Theorie des institutionellen Wandels: Eine neue Sicht der Wirtschaftsge-schichte, Tübingen.

North, D. C. (1992), Institutionen, institutioneller Wandel und Wirtschaftsleistung, Tübingen.

Picot, A. und *M. Fiedler* (2002), Evolution von Institutionen und Management des Wandels, in: Zeitschrift für Betriebswirtschaft, 67. Jg., Erg.-Heft 2/2002, S. 83-94.

Picot, A.; H. Dietl und *E. Franck,* (2002), Organisation, 3. Aufl., Stuttgart.

Picot, A.; H. Freudenberg und *W. Gaßner* (1999), Management von Reorganisationen: Maßschneidern als Konzept für den Wandel, Wiesbaden.

Richter, R. und *E.G. Furubotn* (2003), Neue Institutionenökonomik, Tübingen.

Simon, H. A. (1959), Administrative Behavior: A Study of Decision Making Processes in Administrative Organization, 2. Aufl., New York.

Voigt, S. (2002), Institutionenökonomik, München.

Williamson, O. E. (1991), Comparative Economic Organization: The Analysis of Discrete Structural Alternatives, in: Administrative Science Quarterly, Vol. 36, No. 2, S. 269-296.

Wolff, B. (1995), Organisation durch Verträge: Koordination und Motivation in Unternehmen, Wiesbaden.

II.
Wissenschaftliches Kolloquium

Rolf Hasse und Uwe Vollmer (eds.)
Incentives and Economic Behaviour
Schriften zu Ordnungsfragen der Wirtschaft · Band 76 · Stuttgart · 2005

Credence Goods: The Monopoly Case

Winand Emons

Contents

1. Introduction

This paper is about expert services. Expert services are provided by medical doctors and lawyers as well as by less glorified repair professions like auto mechanics and appliance service-persons. All these professions have in common that typically the seller not only provides the repair services; at the same time, the seller acts as the expert who determines how much treatment is necessary simply because the customer is unfamiliar with the intricacies and peculiarities of the good in question.

Aggravating this special feature is the fact that even ex post consumers can hardly determine the extent of the service that was required ex ante. It is often prohibitively costly to find out whether repairs were really needed or whether necessary treatments were not performed. Brake shoes changed prematurely work in the same way as if the shoes replaced had really been faulty; so does the patient with his appendix removed (un-)necessarily. In contrast, the wisdom tooth may hurt even when it was in perfect condition at the time of the last check-up; toothache need therefore not prove that necessary treatment was not carried out. Since from ex post observations the buyer can never be certain of the quality of the services he has purchased, such services have been termed credence goods (*Darby* and *Karni* 1973).

The information asymmetry between buyer and seller obviously creates strong incentives for opportunistic seller behavior. On the one hand, if there is plenty of money in repair, the seller may recommend treatments that are not necessary. On the other hand, she may not perform an urgently needed repair if other activities are more profitable. The chances of consumers finding out about such fraudulent behavior are typically slim.

To give a few anecdotes where fraud was covered up: In the Swiss Canton of Ticino "ordinary patients" (i.e., the population average) had 33 % more of the seven most important operations than medical doctors and their families. Interestingly enough, lawyers and their beloved have about the same operation frequency as the families of medical doctors (*Domenighetti* et al. 1993). In Switzerland patients with the minimum level of schooling are twice as likely to have their womb or gall-stones removed than patients with a university degree; for hip-joint operations the probability is even 150 % higher. Ordinary children are 80 % more likely to have their tonsils out than children of medical doctors (*Ktip* 05/22/1996). Further empirical evidence from the market for physician services suggests, e.g., that fee-for-service doctors tend to overprescribe while salaried doctors tend to shirk; see *Gaynor* (1994) for a survey of this literature. In the auto-repair business the most expensive German shops charge up to double of what the cheapest garages charge for bodywork without necessarily being any better (*ADAC Motorwelt* 11/92). In the US unnecessary repairs were recommended to car owners by employees of Sears Automotive Centers in 90 % of the test cases (*Wall Street Journal* 6/23/92). Other examples include the life-insurance industry where a New York investigation found the sale of unsuitable policies, high-pressure selling, and unbridled sales expenses (*Newsweek* 2/7/1994), as well as the market for legal advice where the anecdotal evidence is perhaps best summarized by the joke of the longevity study which found that the average lawyer lives twice as long as the average school teacher: Life span for lawyers was computed using billing hours.

Apparently, there is a need for mechanisms to discipline fraudulent experts. Perhaps the simplest mechanism ensuring honest services is the separation of diagnosis and treatment. Unless there is collusion, the diagnosing expert has no incentive to recommend unnecessary treatments and the repairing expert may only fix what has been diagnosed by her colleague. An example of this simple yet effective mechanism is the often encountered separation of the prescription and the preparation of drugs.

This "separation" mechanism, however, fails to do a good job when it is cheaper to provide diagnosis and repair jointly rather than separately. It is, for example, cheaper to repair any damage while the transmission or belly is open for diagnosis than to put everything back together and repeat the process elsewhere for the actual repair. Apparently, such economies of scope between diagnosis and repair also make the related mechanism of calling upon a second opinion unattractive.

In this paper we want to analyze whether the market may solve the fraudulent expert problem when there are profound economies of scope between diagnosis and treatment. In our set-up repair is possible only after diagnosis. If a customer were to choose the services of a second expert, he would automatically incur the cost of a further diagnosis which makes the "separation" as well as the "second opinion" mechanisms unattractive.

For expositional convenience we consider a credence good monopolist.[1] The analysis of the monopoly case enables us to highlight the incentive issues involved without obscuring the main points by strategic competition considerations. Our credence good monopolist has to invest in capacity before actually performing diagnosis and repair. This implies that the expert may have to ration her clientele due to insufficient capacity or that she may also end up with idle capacity. The cost of capacity is sunk. The expert charges separate prices for diagnosis and repair.

To understand our results it is quite useful to know what is efficient if there were no information asymmetry between buyers and seller. In such a world with symmetric information the sum of the consumers´ and the producer´s surplus is maximized when the seller is honest and sets capacity to the level allowing her to satisfy the entire demand by means of non-fraudulent services.

---

[1] We do not need a monopolist in the market structure sense. High information and search costs to consumers, which do definitely exist with credence goods, often provide a source of imperfect competition. A nice example is *Chadwick*'s analysis of funeral provisions in England in the 19th century, when there were about 600-700 undertakers in London to provide 120 funerals per day. *Chadwick* argues that supply-side competitiveness was thwarted by demand-side characteristics such as high search costs and led to monopoly-like conditions over each funeral service, see, e.g., *Ekelund* and *Price* (1979). Moreover, note that since we deal with a credence goods monopolist, the "separation" and the "second opinion" mechanisms described in the preceding paragraph cannot work simply for lack of a second expert.

Next, suppose that in our set-up with asymmetric information consumers infer the seller's behavior from ex ante observations. This, in fact, implies that the seller cannot gain anything by cheating: consumers will detect fraud beforehand and their willingness-to-pay for the services is lower than if the seller were honest. Consequently, the best the seller can hope for is to appropriate the surplus that is generated by honest behavior. To achieve this, she has to persuade consumers of her non-fraudulent services. It remains to be explained how consumers infer the seller's incentives.

We start our analysis with the case where the expert's diagnosis and repair services are observable and verifiable, i.e., buyers observe how much diagnosis and repair they get, yet they have no idea how much of it is actually necessary. First, we consider the situation in which consumers observe the expert's capacity choice. With observability the expert can commit herself to a certain capacity level to convince consumers of her honest repair policy. We analyze how the expert's incentives depend on the interplay of prices, capacity, and the size of her clientele. If, say, the expert does not have enough customers, she may carry out unnecessary repairs to utilize her otherwise idle capacity; with too many customers she may repair inefficiently little if diagnosis is more profitable than treatment.

We show that in equilibrium the expert picks the capacity level allowing her to serve the whole market with honest behavior. Given that she has committed herself to this capacity level, all prices under which diagnosis is at least as profitable as repair induce non-fraudulent behavior. If diagnosis and repair generate the same profit, the expert is indifferent between the two activities and, accordingly, has no incentive to cheat. If diagnosis is more profitable than repair, the expert wishes to increase the number of diagnoses at the expense of repairs. Yet if she diagnoses all products, the only way to use up the capacity she committed herself to is by carrying out non-fraudulent repair. The expert sets the price level so as to appropriate the entire surplus. Consequently, all equilibria of this game share the following features: the expert sets capacity so as to serve the whole market with non-fraudulent behavior. All consumers consult the expert who, in turn, is honest. The equilibria are, therefore, efficient. The expert appropriates the entire surplus.

In a next step we analyze to what extent these nice efficiency properties depend on the fact that the expert can commit herself to a certain capacity level. To do this we consider a second scenario in which capacity is unobservable. With unobservable capacity the expert's incentive structure changes rather drastically. It is no longer the relative profitability of diagnosis to repair which plays the major role in determining behavior; now the price per repair relative to the capacity cost crucially determines the expert's incentives. If, say, the price per repair exceeds its costs, the expert will "fix" all products she can get hold of. She cannot use the capacity level to commit herself not to do such nasty things.

It turns out that our game with unobservable capacity has a unique equilibrium. Per repair the expert charges a price that equals its cost. With this price the expert is indifferent between fixing and not fixing a product and, therefore, has proper incentives concerning repair. Per diagnosis she charges a price enabling her to appropriate the entire surplus. With these two prices the expert wishes to diagnose all products and to repair only the defective ones. Accordingly, she picks the capacity level allowing her to serve the entire market with non-fraudulent behavior. All consumers consult the expert who, in turn, is honest. Consequently, the equilibrium of the game with unobservable capacity has the same welfare properties as the equilibria of the game with observable capacity. Loosely speaking, by dropping the assumption of observability of the capacity, we reduce the set of equilibria.

Then we turn to the case in which the expert's diagnosis and repair services are unobservable, i.e., consumers neither know how much service they need nor how much service they actually get. With unobservable services the expert has yet another possibility to defraud her customers: She can charge for diagnoses and repairs that she never performed. Here we also start with the case where consumers observe the expert's capacity choice. Since consumers cannot observe the expert's services, her billing policy is in fact independent of her service policy. This also implies that the expert's incentives to provide services do not depend on prices. In equilibrium she charges each customer for a diagnosis and a repair.

If the expert has chosen the capacity level allowing her to efficiently serve the market, there is nothing she can do with this capacity but to provide honest services. In equilibrium the expert commits herself to this capacity level and consumers know that they get honest diagnosis and treatment. Accordingly, in equilibrium the expert overcharges but provides efficient service.

Finally, we consider the case where services and capacity are unobservable. Here the market mechanism no longer solves the fraudulent expert problem. The expert charges each customer and at the same time provides no service. If she has customers, reducing the service rate to zero increases profits. Consumers anticipate this dominant strategy and, in turn, do not consult the expert in the first place. Accordingly, no trade takes place.

The extent of the theoretical literature on fraudulent experts is fairly small. In a classic article *Darby* and *Karni* (1973) discuss how reputation, market conditions, and technological factors affect the amount of fraud. Their paper relies heavily on verbal arguments and anecdotes. Yet it contains some of the ideas we formalize in the paper at hand. *Demski* and *Sappington* (1987) focus on the problem of inducing an expert to acquire a costly expertise. While in our model diagnosis is necessary prior to repair, "blind treatment" is possible in *Demski* and *Sappington*; repair is assumed to be costless. In this set-up they study optimal contracts between a principal and an expert (agent).

Pitchik and *Schotter* (1987) describe a mixed-strategy equilibrium in an expert-customer game. The expert randomizes between either reporting truthfully or not; the customer randomizes between acceptance and rejection of a treatment recommendation. *Wolinsky* (1993) examines customer search for multiple opinions and reputation considerations. In his specialization equilibrium some experts exclusively provide diagnosis while the other experts engage in either activity. Consumers first visit a "diagnosis-only" expert. If she recommends treatment, consumers visit a "two-activity" expert for a second diagnosis and the actual repair. *Taylor* (1995) considers experts who may recommend unnecessary treatments. His experts never diagnose a product as healthy; moreover, ex post contracting, free diagnostic checks, consumer procrastination in obtaining checkups, and long-term maintenance agreements may occur in *Taylor's* equilibria.

The major difference between the paper at hand and *Pitchik* and *Schotter* (1987), *Wolinsky* (1993), and *Taylor* (1995) is that they all (implicitly) assume unnecessary repairs to be costless whereas our expert needs resources for unnecessary treatments. This implies that overtreatment is always profitable in their set-up. In contrast, the profitability of overtreatment in our model depends on demand conditions and is determined endogenously. Moreover, they assume the problem of undertreatment away while we solve both, the problems of over- and undertreatment simultaneously.

In *Emons* (1997) we consider experts engaging in *Bertrand-Edgeworth* competition. We show that a market equilibrium exists in which experts are honest and all the surplus goes to consumers. The two papers differ in the following important respects. While the first paper deals only with the case of observable services together with observable capacity, here we also allow for unobservable services and/or unobservable capacity. Moreover, here we analyze credence goods monopolists whereas the other paper is about competitive experts. Nevertheless, the two papers are related in their basic result: if consumers rationally process ex ante information, the market mechanism can solve the fraudulent expert problem.[2] The paper at hand draws heavily on *Emons* (2001).

The remainder of the paper is organized as follows. In section 2. we analyze observable services. In section 2.1. we describe the basic model. Section 2.2. deals with the case of observable capacity while in section 2.3. we analyze the scenario with unobservable capacity. Section 3. is about unobservable services. After describing the model, in section 3.2. we analyze observable and in section 3.3. unobservable capacity. Section 4. concludes the paper. Proofs are relegated to the Appendix.

---

[2] Other related theoretical papers include *Milgrom* and *Roberts* (1986), *Glazer* and *McGuire* (1991), *Pitchik* and *Schotter* (1993), *Dana* and *Spier* (1993), *Wolinsky* (1995), *Dulleck* (1998), *Alger* and *Salanié* (2001), *Emons* (2001), *Liebi* (2002a and 2002b), and *Pesendorfer* and *Wolinsky* (2003). For an experimental study mimicking a market for expertise, see *Plott* and *Wilde* (1991). There is also a small empirical literature on credence goods. *Ekelund* et al. (1995) and *Mixon* (1995) extend an approach of *Laband* (1986) to classify search and experience goods to include credence goods. They show that sellers of credence goods provide more informational cues such as certification and licensing in the *Yellow Pages* than do sellers of search goods. *Laband* (1991) argues that price may work to proxy experience and credence goods.

2. Observable Expert Services

2.1. The Model

We consider a durable good endowed with a stock of services. When a certain amount of services is left over, the product is up for diagnosis and potential repair. We normalize this remaining capacity to 1 monetary unit. During its remaining life, our durable is of the "one-hoss shay" type, i.e., either it makes available total remaining services 1 or it delivers services 0.

When the product is up for diagnosis, it can be either in good or in bad shape. If the product is in good shape, it makes available services 1 with probability $q_h \in (0,1)$; when the product is in bad shape, the corresponding probability is q_l with $0 < q_l < q_h$. Accordingly, in either condition the product may work or fail. Yet when it is in good shape, the probability of making available total capacity is higher. Let p denote the probability that the product is in bad and $(1 - p)$ the probability of the product being in good shape. The consumer does not know in which of the two conditions his product is.

The expert, however, is able to detect the product's condition. By diagnosing the product, the expert finds out whether it is in good or in bad shape. When the product is in bad shape the expert can fix it so that it is in good shape afterwards. Let $d > 0$ be the total resource cost of diagnosing a product; the total resource cost of a repair is $r > 0$.

The timing of the production decisions, however, is such that these costs are not experienced as genuine marginal costs. The expert makes a prior capacity choice. More specifically, the expert chooses $L \geq 0$ units capacity, say hours of time. If she does not invest this time in the expertise business, she can work the L hours in an alternative job. If she does enter the expert business with capacity L, she allocates the L units of time to diagnosis and repair; d is the time an expert needs per diagnosis and r the time per repair. An expert's capacity cost, however, is sunk. Once she has picked capacity L for the expertise business, she can only use these hours for diagnosis and repair; this time is no longer available for the alternative job.

The expert's reservation wage is normalized to 1. Accordingly, L is the sunk cost of the capacity choice; d and r measure the minimum average costs of diagnosis and repair if, say, the expert performs either activity exclusively. Note that marginal costs are different from average costs. The expert has fixed capacity the cost of which is sunk. Therefore, her marginal costs are 0 except for the capacity margin where marginal costs are " $+\infty$ ". When we talk about minimum average costs in the following, we mean d and r.

There is a continuum of identical consumers with total measure 1.[3] Consumers are risk neutral and care only about monetary flows. Accordingly, given that we have normalized the product's remaining capacity to 1 monetary unit, without diagnosis and repair a consumer's expected utility is $\bar{U} = (1 - p)\, q_h + pq_l$. With (honest) diagnosis and repair priced at minimum average costs the consumer's expected utility amounts to $q_h - d - pr$. The consumer incurs the cost of diagnosis in any case. With probability p the product is in bad shape and needs treatment. In return the consumer has a product that is in good shape for sure.

It is efficient to check the product and fix it if necessary, meaning $q_h - d - pr > \bar{U}$ or $p(q_h - q_l) > d + pr$. Fixing a bad product increases the consumer's utility by $(q_h - q_l)$. With probability p the product is in bad shape. Accordingly, the expected benefit from diagnosing and repairing the product is $p(q_h - q_l)$. The surplus the expert's services may generate, therefore, is $W := p(q_h - q_l) - (d + pr)$. For notational purposes we also define the ratio of benefit to costs $w := p(q_h - q_l)/(d + pr)$.

We assume that repair is possible only after diagnosis.[4] Given non-fraudulent behavior, the expert's capacity L in units of time thus translates into the capacity $L/(d + pr)$ in terms of customers.

Let us now describe how the expert may defraud consumers. The consumer does not know in which condition the product is. Later when consuming the remaining services he learns whether his product will work or fail. Yet, a good product may break down and a bad product may work satisfactorily. Accordingly, the consumer cannot use the information about his product's future performance to infer its condition at the time when it was up for diagnosis and repair.

After diagnosis the expert knows in which condition the product is. When the product is in bad shape, she can repair it, i.e., turn it into good shape. Yet she can also "repair" a good product; in this case the expert unnecessarily works r units of time on the product – leaving it at least in good shape. Alternatively, when the product is in good condition, the expert can recommend not to fix it. Nevertheless, she can make the same recommendation when the product is in bad shape. Ex post the consumer has no

---

[3] We make the continuum assumption not only for notational convenience. With a finite number of consumers we run into the following problem. Suppose the expert expects a clientele with $(1 - p)$ good and p bad products. With a finite number of customers, however, the actual realization of her clientele will be different from the expected one. Accordingly, at the end of the day she will realize that she has either too little or excess capacity and she will start behaving fraudulently (suggesting that it is better to see an expert in the morning rather than late afternoon). With a continuum of customers we do not encounter this difficultly which would complicate the analysis substantially. Yet in such a more general set-up, if appropriately modelled our qualitative results should still hold in expectation.

[4] This is the standard assumption made in literature; see, e.g., *Nitzan* and *Tzur* (1991), *Wolinsky* (1993), or *Taylor* (1995). It captures in a straightforward manner the idea that it is cheaper to provide dignosis and repair jointly rather than separately. An exception is the paper by *Demski* and *Sappington* (1987).

way of finding out whether his product was repaired unnecessarily or whether it needed treatment that was not provided. The expert's services thus constitute „credence" goods as distinct from search and experience goods – from ex post observations the consumer can never be certain of the quality of the services he has purchased. The only possibility for the consumer not to be defrauded is to infer the expert's incentives to be honest from ex ante observable variables such as the quoted prices and size of the clientele.[5]

The expert picks prices D and R that she charges for diagnosis and repair. Moreover, she chooses a repair policy conditional on the product's condition. We identify this policy by the probability of repair. Let α denote the probability of repair given that the product is in good shape and β the probability of treatment if the product is in bad shape. These two conditional probabilities determine the unconditional ex ante probability of repair $\gamma = (1 - p)\alpha + p\beta$ which is quite useful for later purposes.

With this notation we may distinguish three scenarios. If $\alpha = 0$, $\beta = 1$, and thus $\gamma = p$ we talk of *efficient repair*. The expert fixes all bad and no good products; thereafter a product is certainly in good shape. A consumer's expected utility with this honest repair policy is $q_h - D - pR$.

If $\alpha > 0$, $\beta = 1$, and thus $\gamma = (1 - p)\alpha + p$ we talk of *too much repair*. The expert not only fixes all bad but also good products. With this fraudulent repair policy a consumer's expected utility amounts to $q_h - D - \gamma R$. Obviously, at the same prices the consumer prefers efficient repair to too much repair.

Finally, if $\alpha = 0$, $\beta < 1$, and thus $\gamma = \beta p$ we will talk of *too little repair*. The expert fixes no good and not all bad products. With this deceitful repair policy a product may be in bad shape and the consumer's expected utility is $(1 - p + \gamma)q_h + (p - \gamma)q_l - D - \gamma R$. The consumer prefers efficient to too little repair if $(q_h - q_l) \geq R$ which must be satisfied since $(q_h - q_l)$ is the consumer's reservation utility for repair if the product is in bad shape. If the expert is indifferent between honest and fraudulent behavior, she behaves

---

[5] The fraudulent expert problem may disappear if consumers were to purchase long term insurance contracts that fully cover all repairs *and* forgone services during the entire product life; such covenants are commonly known as service or health maintenance plans. With these contracts experts have correct incentives since they bear all marginal costs; they are the residual claimants. Yet such long term insurance contracts are particularly prone to consumer moral hazard so that in equilibrium consumers may purchase no service maintenance plans. The problem of too little repair may be solved by a short term warranty for lost services: if the product fails, the expert pays the consumer a sufficiently large amount of money. An honest expert may offer such a warranty at a lower cost than an expert who, say, doesn't repair at all. Such warranties provide experts with an incentive not to cheat. Yet, they may easily fail to do the job when there is consumer moral hazard in the last stage of product life. See *Emons* (1988, 1989). There are still a few other mechanisms dealing with the fraudulent expert problem: reputation for honest services; watchdog agencies verifying service quality etc. These mechanisms work only if there is the possibility of heavily punishing the expert if fraud is detected (they need some kind of repeated interaction) and thus lie outside the scope of our set-up.

honestly. Note that the expert's repair policy defines her capacity in terms of customers $L/(d + \gamma r)$.

Let $\eta \in \{0;1\}$ denote the probability that a consumer goes to the expert.[6] If the expert has no capacity, a consumer picks $\eta = 0$. If she has positive capacity and the consumer is indifferent between consulting and not consulting the expert, he opts for $\eta = 1$. If a consumer is rationed by the expert, he pays nothing yet obtains no services so that he ends up with his reservation utility $\bar{U}$.

Consumers have total mass *1*. Accordingly, η also measures the expert's clientele. If $\eta \leq L/(d + \gamma r)$, the expert has enough capacity to treat her entire clientele. If $\eta > L/(d + \gamma r)$, the expert has more customers than she can handle with her repair policy. In this case she has to ration her customers. The number of customers treated by the expert is thus $min\{\eta;\ L/(d + \gamma r)\}$; her expected profit amounts to $min\{\eta;\ L/(d + \gamma r)\}\ (D + \gamma R)-L$.

The specification of the game depends on whether or not consumers observe the expert's capacity choice. We will present the two different formulations, the solution concept, and the analyses in the following two subsections.

2.2. Observable Capacity

Let us start the analysis with the case in which consumers observe the expert's capacity choice. If this choice is observable, the expert can commit herself to a certain capacity level. This in turn may induce a repair policy that the expert would not have chosen had the capacity level been different. Accordingly, observable capacity is a tool that may help to convince consumers of the expert's good intentions.

We formulate these ideas by a three stage game of perfect information.[7] In the first stage of the game the expert picks (D, R, L). In the second stage consumers observe the quoted prices (D, R) as well as the expert's capacity L. Then each consumer chooses whether or not to go to the expert, i.e., each consumer picks $\eta \in \{0;1\}$. In the third stage the expert observes the consumers' decisions and picks her repair policy α and β.

In stage two consumers have beliefs about the expert's stage three repair policy. Consumers evaluate the expected utility of consulting the expert according to these beliefs. Each consumer chooses η so as to maximize his expected utility. We confine

---

[6] Extending η to a strictly mixed strategy adds nothing to the analysis due to the assumed tie-breaking rules.

[7] Since consumers choose simultaneously in stage two, we have, in fact, a game of "almost perfect" instead of "perfect" information. See, e.g., *Tirole* (1988, pp. 431-432). After stage three payoffs are determined as follows. First, nature chooses whether the product is in good or bad shape. Then players follow their plans of stages one to three. Finally, nature decides whether the product works or fails and the actual payoffs are realized.

our attention to symmetric consumer strategies. The credence goods monopolist chooses prices, capacity, and her repair policy so as to maximize her expected profits.

We focus on subgame perfect equilibria. This means, in particular, that each decision maker acts in a sequentially rational fashion, following a strategy from each point forward that maximizes the expected payoff given the current information and beliefs. In our set-up this implies that the expert's repair policy is indeed optimal once consumers arrive. In equilibrium the consumers' beliefs are borne out: what consumers expect is what experts actually choose to do.

It turns out that the equilibria of our game have a neat structure: The equilibrium capacity is tied down uniquely at the level where the expert can just serve the whole market non-fraudulently. She repairs honestly. All consumers consult the expert and pay prices which enable the expert to appropriate the entire surplus W. Formally, the set of equilibria is given by the following Proposition.

Proposition 1: In a subgame perfect equilibrium in stage one the expert sets $L = (d + pr)$. Furthermore, she charges prices $D \in [dw; p(q_h - q_l)]$ and $R = q_h - q_l - D/p$. In stage two consumers believe that $\alpha = 0$, $\beta = 1$, and choose $\eta = 1$. In stage three the expert picks $\alpha = 0$ and $\beta = 1$.

This result may be explained as follows: Suppose, for the moment, a consumer can deduce the expert's repair policy from the observation of capacity and prices. A consumer is happiest about the expert's services when he is certain to get a product in good shape; the consumer then has the maximum willingness-to-pay of $p(q_h - q_l)$ for the expert's services. The consumer certainly has a good product if the expert repairs efficiently or if she repairs too much. The consumer's overall willingness-to-pay does not increase if the expert raises repair above the efficient level. Yet, if the expert repairs too much, she employs more of her costly time than with efficient repair, without making more money. Accordingly, the expert maximizes her profits by non-fraudulent repair. The maximum prices the consumer is willing to pay for non-fraudulent repair, i.e., the prices generating utility $\hat{U}$ are given by the indifference curve $R = q_h - q_l - D/p$; see Figure 1. With these prices and honest repair the consumer sets $\eta = 1$.

Let us now analyze how the consumer finds out about the expert's repair policy in stage three. Recall that at this stage the expert has capacity L, the cost of which is sunk. In terms of customers the expert has capacity $L/(d + pr)$ given honest behavior. Apparently, the expert's behavior depends on the size of her clientele η relative to her capacity $L/(d + pr)$. If, say, $\eta < L/(d + pr)$, the expert may start "repairing" good products to utilize her otherwise idle capacities. Conversely, if $\eta > L/(d + pr)$, she may, e.g., be tempted not to fix all bad products given that diagnosis is more profitable than repair.

Figure 1:   **Expert's incentives with observable capacity**

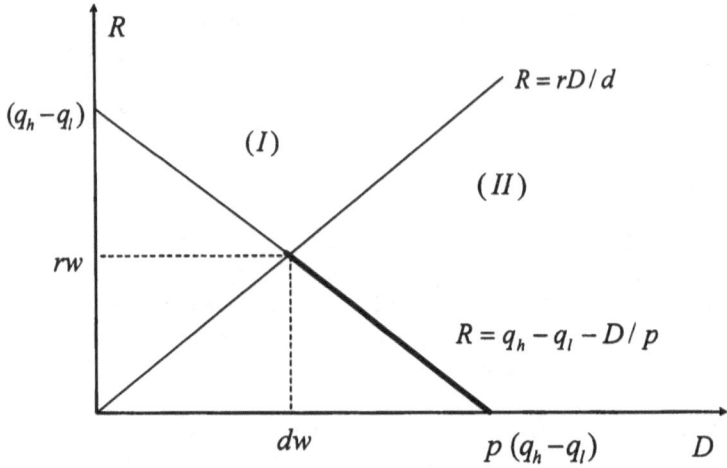

The last example indicates that the expert's incentives also depend on the relative profitability of diagnosis to repair which in turn is determined by her prices D and R. If the expert has too many customers, the only constraint she faces (at the margin) is her precious time. To maximize profits, she compares the profit per hour repair $(R - r)/r$ with the profit per hour diagnosis $(D - d)/d$. If the former exceeds the latter, she will repair too much and vice versa if diagnosis is more profitable than treatment.

To be more specific, consider Figure 1. Along the line $R = rD/d$ we have $(R - r)/r = (D - d)/d$. Accordingly, on this line the expert is indifferent between diagnosis and treatment so that with $\eta \geq L/(d + pr)$ customers she opts for efficient repair.[8] In region (I) where $R > rD/d$ the expert prefers repair to diagnosis. Whatever the number of customers, she will "fix" anything she diagnoses, i.e., repair too much. In region (II) in which $R < rD/d$ the expert prefers diagnosis to repair so that she wishes to increase the number of diagnoses at the expense of repairs. With $\eta = L/(d + pr)$ customers, however, if she diagnoses all products, she uses up her otherwise idle capacity by efficient repair. If $\eta < L/(d + pr)$, the expert has proper incentives if and only if $R = 0$. She does not repair too much to utilize her idle capacity because there is no money in treatment.[9]

---

[8]   In the principal-agent literature a related result is known as the equal compensation principle. See, e.g., *Milgrom* and *Roberts* (1992, pp. 228-232).

[9]   *Darby* and *Karni* (1973) also point out that the sellers' incentives depend on the state of demand. When there is "no customer waiting for service", sellers have an incentive to oversell their services to utilize idle resources; this incentive to oversell disappears when "the lenth of the queue of customers waiting for service is positive". *Darby* and *Karni* do not discuss that the sellers' incentives also depend on prices.

Subgame perfection implies that the consumers' beliefs reflect the expert's incentive structure we have just derived. Note that it is possible to pin down the expert's incentives even further once we incorporate the exact specifications of L and η. We do this in the proof. The most important aspects of the expert's incentives, however, are summarized by the previous discussion.

Finally, note that prices on the lower (heavy) part of the indifference curve $R = q_h - q_l - D/p$, together with the capacity inducing honest repair, give rise to positive profits per customer. Accordingly, to maximize profits the expert chooses $L = d + pr$ so that she serves the entire market with honest behavior. Given this capacity level, all prices on the indifference curve $R = q_h - q_l - D/p$ with $D \in [dw; p(q_h - q_l)]$ support non-fraudulent repair.

2.3. Unobservable Capacity

Let us now turn to the case in which the expert's capacity choice is unobservable. With unobservable capacity the expert cannot commit herself to a certain capacity level to persuade consumers of her honest repair policy. Certain prices that support honesty in the previous set-up will no longer induce non-fraudulent repair if the expert can secretly increase her capacity. As will become clear in the following discussion, observable capacity is like *Cortés* burning his ships upon arrival in Mexico as a commitment not to retreat or like *Odysseus* having himself lashed to the mast and ordering his sailors to plug their ears with wax as a commitment not to go to the *Siren*'s island.

To be more specific, consider, e.g., the prices $D = dw$ and $R = rw$; see Figure 1. These prices, together with the commitment to the capacity $L = d + pr$, induce non-fraudulent repair in the preceding set-up. Note, however, that repair is more profitable than the alternative job, i.e., $R = rw > r$. If the expert can increase the number of repairs at the expense of the time she devotes to the alternative job, clearly she will do it. Accordingly, with the above prices and unobservable capacity consumers should expect the expert to repair all products and to have capacity $L = d + r$.

Let us now tackle the task of modeling unobservable capacity. We want to capture the fact that consumers have not yet seen the expert's capacity choice when they pick η. There are potentially two ways of achieving this: Either we stick to the previous formulation in which the expert picks capacity in stage one and assume that consumers do not observe this choice; or, alternatively, the expert chooses her capacity only in stage three together with the repair policy. Under both formulations consumers do not observe the expert's capacity when they pick η.

While the first formulation may appear more natural, there is a snag to it. When consumers decide, they have beliefs about the expert's capacity choice which has already taken place. Technically, this formulation gives rise to a game of imperfect information. To solve it we need sophisticated solution concepts such as perfect *Bayesian* or sequential equilibria.

If we choose the second formulation, we have once again a game of perfect information. We can solve it using subgame perfect equilibria which, in turn, can be found by simple backwards induction. For this technical reason we opt for the second formulation. Nevertheless, the equilibrium we derive is also an equilibrium for the first formulation with the strategies and beliefs adjusted accordingly.

More specifically, in stage one the expert chooses D and R. In stage two consumers observe these prices and have beliefs about the repair policy *and* the capacity. According to these beliefs consumers evaluate the expected utility with the expert and pick η. In stage three the expert chooses (α, β, L).

It turns out that this game has a unique equilibrium: The expert sets her capacity to the level allowing her to serve the whole market with non-fraudulent behavior. She repairs honestly. All consumers consult the expert. With the price for repair the expert persuades consumers of her honesty; with the price for diagnosis she appropriates the entire surplus W. Formally, the equilibrium is given by the following Proposition.

Proposition 2: In the unique subgame perfect equilibrium in stage one the expert charges $D = p(q_h - q_l) - pr$ and $R = r$. In stage two consumers believe that $\alpha = 0$, $\beta = 1$, $L = d + pr$, and choose $\eta = 1$. In stage three the expert picks $\alpha = 0$, $\beta = 1$, and $L = d + pr$.

This result is driven by the following ideas. Since the expert simultaneously picks her capacity and her repair policy, she will co-ordinate these choices. This means that if she opts for positive capacity, she will exhaust it with her repair policy; she will have neither insufficient nor excess capacity. Put differently, once we know her capacity, we know her repair policy, and vice versa.

Let us first look at the capacity choice. Given an ex ante probability of repair γ, the expert earns $(D + \gamma R)$ per customer at a cost of $(d + \gamma r)$. If the latter exceeds the former, she makes a loss per customer and, accordingly, sets $L = 0$. If the former exceeds the latter, the expertise business is more profitable than the alternative job. The expert sets capacity so as to satisfy the entire demand with her repair policy. Consequently, $L = 0$ for prices below the (heavy) line $D = d + \gamma(r - R)$ whereas for prices above this kinked line $L = \eta [d + \gamma r]$. See Figure 2.

Let us now determine the expert's optimal repair policy. If $R < r$, repair is less attractive than the outside job and, therefore, the expert does not repair at all so that $\gamma = 0$. If $R = r$, the price of a repair equals its minimum average costs. The expert is indifferent and thus repairs efficiently, implying $\gamma = p$. Finally, if $R > r$ the expert repairs anything she can get hold of because repair is more profitable than the alternative job, i.e., $\gamma = 1$. See Figure 2.

Figure 2: **Expert's incentives with unobservable capacity**

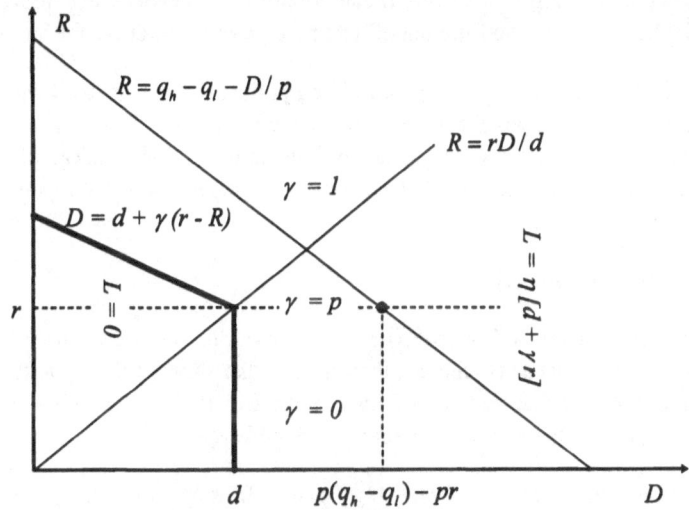

If the expert repairs efficiently or too much, the consumers' willingness-to-pay for the expert's services equals $p(q_h - q_l)$. Efficient repair generates this revenue at a lower cost than too much repair. Consequently, the expert maximizes profits by non-fraudulent repair and she persuades consumers of her honesty by charging $R = r$. She sets $D = p(q_h - q_l) - pr$ so as to appropriate the surplus W.

3. Unobservable Expert Services

So far we have assumed that diagnosis and repair are observable and also verifiable. This assumption is appropriate for, say, dentists whose customers, willy-nilly, suffer any (un-) necessary drilling. It is however inappropriate for, e.g., a customer taking his car to the shop in the morning and picking it up in the evening without being able to tell whether the mechanic has worked on the vehicle. With unobservable services the expert has yet another possibility to defraud her customers: She can claim to have checked and fixed the car without even having looked at it, thus collecting diagnosis and repair fees from an unlimited number of customers.[10]

3.1. The Model

Our previous model is easily extended to be able to cope with unobservable services. First, we have to introduce a diagnosis policy which we capture by the probability of diagnosis $\delta \in [0;1]$. Since a repair is possible only after a diagnosis, the ex ante

---

[10] Note that in *Wolinsky's* (1993) model diagnosis is verifiable and repair is unverifiable.

probability of repair has to be modified to δy. If the expert is indifferent between working and not working, she works; if she is indifferent between underdiagnosis and underrepair she diagnoses too little but efficiently repairs all products she has a look at.

Next we have to introduce the expert's billing policy. By Δ, $\Gamma \in [0;1]$ we denote the probabilities that she charges for a diagnosis or a repair, respectively. Since consumers cannot observe the expert's services, her billing policy is independent of her actual diagnosis and repair policies. Nevertheless, since consumers know that repair is possible only after diagnosis, $\Delta \geq \Gamma$.

3.2. Observable Capacity

We start the analysis of unobservable services with the case where consumers observe the expert's capacity choice. It turns out that observable capacity is such a strong commitment device that in equilibrium the expert provides efficient diagnosis and repair; yet, unless the repair fee is zero, she overcharges.

We consider the following three stage game. In stage one the expert chooses (D, R, L). In stage two consumers observe these choices. They have beliefs about the diagnosis, repair, and billing policies. According to these beliefs consumers evaluate the expected utility with the expert and pick η. In stage three the expert chooses $(\delta, \alpha, \beta, \Delta, \Gamma)$.

Proposition 3: In a subgame perfect equilibrium in stage one the expert sets $L = (d + pr)$. Furthermore, she charges $D \in [0;p(q_h - q_l)]$ and $R = p(q_h - q_l) - D$. In stage two consumers believe that $\delta = 1$, $\alpha = 0$, $\beta = 1$, $\Delta = 1$, $\Gamma = 1$, and choose $\eta = 1$. In stage three the expert picks $\delta = 1$, $\alpha = 0$, $\beta = 1$, $\Delta = 1$, and $\Gamma = 1$.

This result rests on the following reasoning. Since consumers cannot observe the expert's services, her billing policy is independent of her actual diagnosis and repair policy. It is, therefore, a (weakly) dominant strategy to charge each customer for a diagnosis and repair.

Let us now determine her diagnosis and repair policy. First, note that if the expert has positive capacity, there is nothing she can do with it but to diagnose and repair. Thus, if with honest services the number of customers does not exceed her capacity, the expert diagnoses and repairs efficiently. If, on the other hand, she has more customers than she can handle with honest services, only a fraction of her clientele gets treatment.

With honest services the consumers' willingness-to-pay is $p(q_h - q_l)$. Accordingly, if the expert has capacity $L \geq (d + pr)$ and charges prices such that $D + R \leq p(q_h - q_l)$, consumers are happy and consult the expert. The consumers' willingness-to-pay is lower if $L < (d + pr)$ because in this case they do not get treatment for sure. Finally, note that if the expert sets $L = (d + pr)$ and charges prices such that $D + R = p(q_h - q_l)$, she appropriates the entire surplus W.[11]

It is perhaps surprising that the commitment device capacity alone is sufficient to guarantee honest services. If the expert has the efficient capacity level, there is nothing she can do with it but to diagnose and repair efficiently. Since she can charge independently of the services she performs, her incentives do not depend on prices. This observation also explains why it is "easier" to establish Proposition 3 than Proposition 1 where the expert's incentives depend on capacity and prices.

3.3. Unobservable Capacity

Let us now briefly consider the case of unobservable capacity. To do so we change the game of section 3.2. as follows: The expert chooses capacity in stage 3 instead of stage 1; in stage 2 consumers have beliefs about this capacity choice. It is straightforward to see that in any equilibrium of this game the expert has no capacity and, accordingly, provides no services. Whatever the prices and the number of customers, in stage 3 it is a dominant strategy for the expert

– to charge each customer for a diagnosis and a repair,

– to set capacity to zero, and

– to diagnose and repair nothing.

A positive capacity level would increase costs without generating additional revenue.

With unobservable capacity the expert will thus always pick $L = 0$. Since consumers anticipate this behavior, they will not consult the expert in the first place so that we have no trade. Thus, if the expert cannot commit herself to a capacity level, with unobservable services she makes no profit. Consequently, if services and capacity are unobservable, the market mechanism cannot solve the fraudulent expert problem. This last result should help to clarify the central role capacity plays as commitment device in the previous section.

4. Discussion and Conclusions

We have analyzed a credence good which is provided by an expert. Since consumers can never be certain of the quality of the seller's services, the expert has strong incentives to cheat. We have shown that if consumers rationally process all the information about market conditions, they can infer the seller's incentives: In three out

---

[11] It is worth mentioning that if $D = p(q_h - q_l)$ and $R = 0$, trivially any $\Gamma \in [0,1]$ is optimal for the expert. She may thus set $\Gamma = p$ so that in this particular equilibrium she does not overcharge.

of four constellations the market does indeed solve the fraudulent expert problem. Only when services and capacity are unobservable do we end up with a no-trade equilibrium.

These findings corroborate our earlier results (*Emons* 1997). There we show for a competitive framework that a market equilibrium exists in which experts are honest and all the surplus goes to consumers. Accordingly, the message of the two papers is in the same spirit: If consumers rationally process ex ante information about market conditions, the market mechanism can solve the fraudulent expert problem. Experts are honest in order to maximize the consumers' surplus. In the competitive set-up honesty is necessary in order to survive; in the monopoly case non-fraudulent service generates the highest profit for the credence goods monopolist.

A few more remarks seem to be in order. First, note that the possibility of charging separate prices for diagnosis and repair is crucial for our results on honest expert services. If we restrict the price of diagnosis to be zero and allow only the repair fee to be positive, as seems to be common practice at full-repair shops in the US, our model makes the following predictions: With observable services and capacity there is always overtreatment because repair is (infinitely) more profitable than diagnosis. With observable services and unobservable capacity the price of a repair must exceed its average cost to cover the free diagnosis; but then repair is also more profitable than the outside job and the expert will "repair" anything she can get hold of. Only when services are unobservable and capacity is observable there exists an equilibrium with free diagnosis and non-fraudulent services. In this scenario capacity alone serves as an incentive device and efficient services go along with a whole range of prices, including the pricing policy of American full-repair shops.

Second, a comparison between Propositions 1 and 3 sheds some more light on the role of observability of services. With unobservable services the capacity commitment, in and of itself, is sufficient to sustain the efficient outcome. Since the expert charges all customers a repair anyway, her repair policy is completely independent of her pricing policy. Therefore, the relative price of repair and diagnosis doesn't matter at all and the whole range of relative prices from zero to infinity is consistent with honest services. Things are different with observable services. Here the repair and pricing policies are not independent: the expert may only charge for those repairs she actually performed. If repair is more profitable than diagnosis, the expert repairs too much. Accordingly, with observable services the range of prices consistent with non-fraudulent services is "smaller" than with unobservable services.

Third, note that the positive result of Proposition 3 depends crucially on our assumption of zero variable costs up to capacity: once capacity is installed, there is nothing the expert can do with it but work honestly. In contrast, if there were, say, positive variable costs of repair, the expert might try to slash these costs by undertreatment. What are then examples for this cost-structure that is the driving force for our positive result? The most obvious example is the small, owner-operated firm. Our model may thus help to explain why many credence goods are provided by owner-operated firms. If the firm grows and services are provided by employees instead of the owner herself, the prediction depends on whether wages constitute a variable cost or not. If wages are a fixed cost in the short run, as is typically the case in Europe, our cost structure is a reasonable approximation of a firm with employees; if, however, hire and fire policies are the rule, wages are a variable cost and capacity alone can no longer commit the seller to provide efficient services. In such a situation partnerships might be an attempt to mimic the cost structure that is necessary for capacity to work as a commitment device.

Our next remarks concern the interpretation of capacity. A legal practice of two lawyers has (approximately) double the capacity of a one-woman-firm. A plumber with 20 employees has a much higher capacity than her colleague working with an apprentice only. If capacity is, say, an X-ray machine (the opportunity cost of which is its price), even an ordinary patient has an idea whether this machine can handle 5 or 50 patients a day. The important ratio clientele/capacity may be proxied simply by how crowded the shop typically is.

Fourth, a few remarks for the empirically-inclined reader. As a first approximation, the important ratio clientele/capacity may be proxied simply by how crowded the shop typically is. Empirical tests of the theoretical results are extremely difficult due to the very nature of the problem: it is fraud that we are looking for. Nevertheless, *Marty* (1998) shows using 8000 bills of Swiss general practitioners that busy doctors charge significantly less per patient than doctors with insufficient demand, indicating that there is indeed demand inducement. *Keeler* and *Fok* (1996) study the impact of an insurance reform in California that, after higher reimbursements for cesarean deliveries, equalized fees for vaginal and cesarean delivery, a relative price shift of 21 %. They found a 0.7 % nonsignificant drop of cesarean rates. This result, which doesn't appear consistent with the result of Proposition 1, may perhaps be explained by other high powered incentive devices such as medical malpractice suits that certainly discipline medical doctors in California. Interestingly enough, despite their result *Keeler* and *Fok* (1996) recommend the equalization of fees because it need not hurt providers and may improve patient trust.

In a simple framework we were able to work out conditions under which the market mechanism can solve the fraudulent expert problem. For a lot of skilled trades offering services of credence quality the market mechanism actually seems to do a fairly good job just as our model predicts; at least we couldn't find any anecdotes of, say, cheating plumbers, electricians, or cobblers.[12] In other professions, as the examples in the Introduction suggest, there is, however, fraud. The majority of these examples is from the medical profession where the market certainly does not operate in such an

---

[12] See also *Plott* and *Wilde* (1982, p. 99) who were "amazed" by how well the market did in their experiments. They conclude that markets as social control devices cannot be dismissed a priori.

unhampered way as is assumed in our model; prices are often set by a regulator rather than the seller, insurers pay for the services, distorting consumers' incentives to gather and process the necessary information, etc. Accordingly, these examples of fraud do not contradict our analysis. Perhaps our results may help to find out what goes wrong in these professions so that better mechanism can be designed to induce honest services. Since expert services are often subject to licensing and regulation, a more thorough understanding of these markets will be helpful for public policy purposes. For credence goods sellers the following strategy recommendations follow from our analysis: With the cost structure given in the paper it is possible to convince rational consumers of the quality of your services and to make a lot of money. Therefore, try to mimic this cost structure by setting up, e.g., a partnership; moreover, try to commit to a sunk capacity, in particular if your services are unobservable.

Appendix

1. Proof of Proposition 1:

We solve the game by backwards induction.

a) If $1 > L/(d + pr)$, the expert has more customers than she can handle with honest behavior. Given her time constraint, she is only interested in the profit per hour repair $(R - r)/r$ compared to the profit per hour diagnosis $(D - d)/d$.

If $R = rD/d$ which implies $(R - r)/r = (D - d)/d$, the expert is indifferent between diagnosis and repair and, therefore, repairs honestly. Accordingly, she sets $\alpha = 0$, $\beta = 1$ so that $\gamma = p$. A consumer who is served has utility $q_h - D - pR$. The consumer buys, i.e., sets $\eta = 1$, if prices do not exceed $D = dw$ and $R = rw$. With these maximum prices that consumers still accept the expert makes profits:

$$(L/(d + pr)) [D + pR] - L = (L/(d + pr)) [p(q_h - q_l) - (d + pr)] < W$$

because $L/(d + pr) < 1$.

If $R > rD/d$, the expert prefers repair to diagnosis. She sets $\alpha = \beta = \gamma = 1$ and thus treats $L/(d + r)$ customers. A consumer who is served has utility $q_h - D - R$. The maximum prices the consumer is willing to pay are $D \in [0;dw)$ and $R = p(q_h - q_l) - D$. With these prices the expert makes profits:

$$(L/(d + r)) [D + R] - L = (L/(d + r)) [p(q_h - q_l) - (d + r)] < W$$

because $L/(d + r) < 1$ and $(d + r) > (d + pr)$.

If $R < rD/d$, the expert prefers diagnosis to repair. She diagnoses all products and repairs only to use her otherwise idle capacity. Accordingly, she sets

$$\gamma = \begin{cases} (L - \eta d)/\eta r, & \text{if } L/(d + pr) < \eta < L/d; \\ 0, & \text{otherwise.} \end{cases}$$

A consumer who is served has utility $q_h - (p - \gamma)(q_h - q_l) - D - \gamma R$. The maximum prices the consumer is willing to pay are $D \in [(q_h - q_l)/(r/d + 1/\gamma); \gamma(q_h - q_l)]$ and $R = (q_h - q_l) - D/\gamma$. With these prices the expert makes profits:

$$(L/(d + \gamma r))[D + \gamma R] - L = (L/(d + \gamma r)) [\gamma (q_h - q_l) - (d + \gamma r)] < W$$

because $r < (q_h - q_l)$ and $L/(d + \gamma r) < 1$.

b) If $1 = L/(d + pr)$, the expert fully uses her capacity with non-fraudulent behavior. If $R < rD/d$, she strictly prefers diagnosis to repair. If she carries out diagnoses for her entire clientele, she has $(L - \eta d)$ units of time left; honestly repairing the bad products just exhausts her capacity. If $R = rD/d$, the expert is honest, the argument being along similar lines as in a). Thus if $R \leq rD/d$, we have $\gamma = p$. A consumer has utility $q_h - D - pR$. The maximum prices a consumer is willing to pay are $D \in [dw; p(q_h - q_l)]$ and $R = q_h - q_l - D/p$. With these prices the expert makes profits:

$$(L/(d + pr)) [D + pR] - L = (L/(d + pr)) [p(q_h - q_l) - (d + pr)] = W$$

because $L/(d + pr) = 1$.

If $R > rD/d$, the expert prefers repair to diagnosis. She sets $\gamma = 1$ and treats only $L/(d + r)$ customers. A consumer who is served has utility $q_h - D - R$. The maximum prices he is willing to pay are $D \in [0; dw)$ and $R = p(q_h - q_l) - D$. With these prices the expert makes profits $(L/(d + r)) [D + R] - L = (L/(d + r)) [p(q_h - q_l) - (d + r)] < W$ because $L/(d + r) < 1$ and $(d + r) > (d + pr)$.

c) If $1 < L/(d + pr)$, the expert has unused capacity with non-fraudulent behavior. If $R > rD/d$, she repairs anything. Accordingly, she sets $\gamma = 1$ and treats $min[L/(d + r); 1]$ customers. A consumer who is served has utility $q_h - D - R$. The maximum prices he is willing to pay are $D \in [0; dw)$ and $R = p(q_h - q_l) - D$. With these prices the expert makes profits:

$$min[L/(d + r); 1][D + R] - L \leq (L/(d + r)) [D + R] - L = $$
$$(L/(d + r)) [p(q_h - q_l) - (d + r)] < W$$

because $L/(d + r) \leq 1$ and $(d + r) > (d + pr)$.

If $0 < R \leq rD/d$, the expert prefers diagnosis to repair. She diagnoses all products and uses repairs to exhaust her remaining capacity. Accordingly, she sets:

$$\gamma = \begin{cases} 1, & \text{if } 1 \leq L/(d + r); \\ (L - \eta d)/\eta r & \text{if } L/(d + r) < 1 < L/d. \end{cases}$$

A consumer has utility $q_h - D - \gamma R$. The maximum prices he is willing to pay are $D \in [p(q_h - q_l)/(1 + \gamma r/d); p(q_h - q_l)]$ and $R = [p(q_h - q_l) - D]/\gamma$. With these prices the expert makes profits:

$$min[L/(d + \gamma r); 1] [D + \gamma R] - L \leq (L/(d + \gamma r)) [p(q_h - q_l) - (d + \gamma r)] < W$$

because $(d + \gamma r) > (d + pr)$ and $L/(d + \gamma r) \leq 1$.

If $R = 0$, the expert sets $\gamma = p$ because there is no money in repair. With this repair policy a consumer has utility $q_h - D$. The maximum prices he is willing to pay are $D = p(q_h - q_l)$ and $R = 0$. With these prices the expert makes profits $D - L < W$ because $1 < L/(d + pr)$.

d) For all other prices the consumers' utility is less than their reservation utility and, accordingly, $\eta = 0$. The expert makes a loss L.

e) If the expert chooses $L = d + pr$, $D \in [dw; p(q_h - q_l)]$ and $R = q_h - q_l - D/p$ she makes the maximum profit W.

Q.E.D.

2. Proof of Proposition 2:

We solve the game by backwards induction.

Stage 3) Given D, R, η, the triple (L, α, β) generates profits:

$$min\{L/(d + \gamma r); \eta\}[D + \gamma R] - L.$$

If $(D + \gamma R)/(d + \gamma r) < 1$, the alternative job is more attractive and the expert sets $L = 0$; if the inequality is reversed, the expertise business is more attractive and the expert sets $L = \eta [d + \gamma r]$ so as to satisfy the entire demand. A capacity in excess of demand is a waste of money.

Next we determine the expert's optimal repair policy. If $R < r$, repair does not cover minimum average cost and the expert sets $\alpha = \beta = \gamma = 0$. If $R = r$, price equals minimum average costs. The expert is indifferent and sets $\alpha = 0$, $\beta = 1$, and thus $\gamma = p$ so that she repairs efficiently. If $R > r$, the expert sets $\alpha = \beta = \gamma = 1$ because repair is more profitable than the outside job.

Stage 2) If the prices are such that $L = 0$, consumers set $\eta = 0$. Now consider those prices with $L = \eta[d + \gamma r]$ so that the entire demand is satisfied. If $R \geq r$, which implies $\gamma \in \{p; 1\}$, the consumer's expected utility amounts to $q_h - D - \gamma R$. The consumer buys, i.e., sets $\eta = 1$, if prices do not exceed $R = [p(q_h - q_l) - D]/\gamma$. For $R < r$ and thus $\gamma = 0$ the consumer's utility is $\bar{U} - D$. He purchases if and only if $D = 0$.

Stage 1) Prices with $R < r$ give rise to zero profits. If for $R \geq r$ the expert charges the maximum prices $R = [p(q_h - q_l) - D]/\gamma$, she makes revenue $p(q_h - q_l)$. For $R = r$ the expert generates this revenue with capacity $L = d + pr$ while for $R > r$ she needs capacity $L = d + r$. Consequently, the expert maximizes her profits by charging $D = p(q_h - q_l) - pr$ and $R = r$.

Q.E.D.

3. Proof of Proposition 3:

We solve the game by backwards induction.

Stage 3) Given (D, R, L, η), the policies $(\delta, \alpha, \beta, \Delta, \Gamma)$ generate profits $\min\{L/\delta(d + \gamma r); \eta\}[\Delta D + \gamma R] - L$. Independently of (δ, α, β), the billing policy $\Delta = \Gamma = 1$ maximizes profits. These choices are unique unless L, η, D, and/or R is zero. Then any Δ and/or $\Gamma \in [0;1]$ is optimal.

Let us now determine the optimal diagnosis and repair policy. If $\eta > L/(d + pr)$, the expert has more customers than she can handle with honest services. She sets $\delta = L/\eta(d + pr) < 1$ and $\alpha = 0$ and $\beta = 1$.

If $\eta \leq L/(d + pr)$, with honest services the expert has at least as much capacity as customers. She sets $\delta = 1$, $\alpha = 0$, $\beta = 1$; overcapacity idles.

Stage 2) If $1 \leq L/(d + pr)$, a customer gets honest services but is overcharged. His utility is thus $q_h - D - R$. The consumer buys, i.e., sets $\eta = 1$, if $D + R \leq p(q_h - q_l)$.

If $1 > L/(d + pr)$, the expert undertreats and overcharges. A consumer's utility is $q_h - (1 - \delta)p(q_h - q_l) - D - R$. The consumer buys if $\delta p(q_h - q_l) \geq D + R$.

Stage 1) If the expert sets $L \geq (d + pr)$ and charges reservation prices $D + R = p(q_h - q_l)$, $\eta = 1$ and the expert's profit is $p(q_h - q_l) - L$. By setting $L = (d + pr)$ the expert maximizes this profit and appropriates the entire surplus W.

If she picks $L < (d + pr)$ and charges the corresponding reservation prices $D + R = \delta p(q_h - q_l)$, $\eta = 1$ and her profit amounts to $\delta p(q_h - q_l) - L = \delta[p(q_h - q_l) - (d + pr)] < W$.

Q.E.D.

References

Alger, Ingela and *François Salanié* (2001), Competitive Pricing of Expert Services: Equilibrium Fraud and Partial Specialization, Discussion Paper, Boston College.

Dana, James and *Kathryn Spier* (1993), Expertise and Contingent Fees: The Role of Asymmetric Information in Attorney Compensation, in: Journal of Law, Economics, and Organization, Vol. 9, pp. 349-367.

Darby, Michael and *Edi Karni* (1973), Free Competition and the Optimal Amount of Fraud, in: Journal of Law and Economics, Vol. 16, pp. 67-88.

Demski, Joel and *David Sappington* (1987), Delegated Expertise, in: Journal of Accounting Research, Vol. 25, pp. 68-89.

Domenighetti, Gianfranco; Antoine Casabianca; Felix Gutzwiller and *Sebastiano Martinoli* (1993), Revisiting the Most Informed Consumer of Surgical Services, in: International Journal of Technology Assessment in Health Care, Vol. 9, pp. 505-513.

Dulleck, Uwe (1998), The Credence Goods Monopoly Problem, Dept. of Econ., Discussion Paper, Humboldt University, Berlin.

Ekelund, Robert and *Edward Price* (1979), Sir Edwin Chadwick on Competition and the Social Control of Industry: Railroads, in: History of Political Economy, Vol. 11, pp. 213-239.

Ekelund, Robert; Franklin Mixon and *Rand Ressler* (1995), Advertising and Information: An Empirical Study of Search, Experience and Credence Goods, in: Journal of Economic Studies, Vol. 22, pp. 33-43.

Emons, Winand (1988), Warranties, Moral Hazard, and the Lemons Problem, in: Journal of Economic Theory, Vol. 46, pp. 16-33.

Emons, Winand (1989), On the Limitation of Warranty Duration, in: Journal of Industrial Economics, Vol. 37, pp. 287-301.

Emons, Winand (1997), Credence Goods and Fraudulent Experts, in: Rand Journal of Economics, Vol. 28, pp. 107-119.

Emons, Winand (2000), Expertise, Contingent Fees, and Insufficient Attorney Effort, in: International Review of Law and Economics, Vol. 20, pp. 21-33.

Emons, Winand (2001), Credence Goods Monopolists, in: International Journal of Industrial Organization, Vol. 19, pp. 375-389.

Gaynor, Martin (1994), Issues in the Industrial Organization of the Market for Physician Services, in: Journal of Economics and Management Strategy, Vol. 3, pp. 211-255.

Glazer, Jacob and *Thomas McGuire* (1991), The Economics of Referrals, Discussion Paper 20, Industry Studies Program, Department of Economics, Boston University.

Keeler, Emmett and *Thomas Fok* (1996), Equalizing Physician Fees Had Little Effect on Cesarean Rates, in: Medical Care Research and Review, Vol. 53, pp. 465-471.

Laband, David (1986), Advertising as Information: An Empirical Note, in: Review of Economics and Statistics, Vol. 68, pp. 517-521.

Laband, David (1991), An Objective Measure of Search versus Experience Goods, in: Economic Inquiry, Vol. 29, pp. 497-509.

Liebi, Thomas (2002a), Trusting Labels: A Matter of Numbers?, Discussion Paper Department of Economics, University of Bern, http://www.vwi.unibe.ch/staff/liebi/label2.pdf.

Liebi, Thomas (2002b), Monitoring Eco-Labels: You Can Have Too Much of a Good Thing, Discussion Paper Department of Economics, University of Bern, http://www.vwi.unibe.ch/staff/liebi/eco-labels.pdf.

Marty, Fridolin (1998), Capacity as a Determinant of the Supply for Physicians' Services, Discussion Paper 05-98, Department of Economics, University of Bern, http://www.vwi.unibe.ch/wpapers/marty/phy_0598.pdf.

Milgrom, Paul and *John Roberts* (1986), Relying on the Information of Interested Parties, in: Rand Journal of Economics, Vol. 17, pp. 18-32.

Milgrom, Paul and *John Roberts* (1992), Economics, Organization and Management, Upper Saddle River.

Mixon, Franklin (1995), Advertising as Information: Further Evidence, in: Southern Economic Journal, Vol. 61, pp. 1213-1218.

Nitzan, Shmuel and *Joseph Tzur* (1991), Costly Diagnosis and Price Dispersion, in: Economics Letters, Vol. 36, pp. 245-251.

Pesendorfer, Wolfgang and *Asher Wolinsky* (2003), Second Opinions and Price Competition: Inefficiency in the Market for Expert Advice, in: Review of Economic Studies, Vol. 70, pp. 417-433.

Pitchik, Carolyn and *Andrew Schotter* (1987), Honesty in a Model of Strategic Information Transmission, in: American Economic Review, Vol. 77, pp. 1032-1036; Errata, in: American Economic Review, Vol. 78 (1988), pp. 1164.

Pitchik, Carolyn and *Andrew Schotter* (1993), Information Transmission in Regulated Markets, in: Canadian Journal of Economics, Vol. 26, pp. 815-829.

Plott, Charles and *Louis Wilde* (1991), Professional Diagnosis vs. Self-Diagnosis: An Experimental Examination of some special Features of Markets with Uncertainty, in: *V. Smith* (ed.), Research in Experimental Economics, Vol. 2, Greenwich/Conn., pp. 63-112.

Taylor, Curtis (1995), The Economics of Breakdowns, Checkups, and Cures, in: Journal of Political Economy, Vol. 103, pp. 53-74.

Tirole, Jean (1988), The Theory of Industrial Organization, Cambridge/Mass.

Wolinsky, Asher (1993), Competition in a Market for Informed Expert Services, in: Rand Journal of Economics, Vol. 24, pp. 380-398.

Wolinsky, Asher (1995), Competition in Markets for Credence Goods, in: Journal of Institutional and Theoretical Economics, Vol. 151, pp. 117-131.

Rolf Hasse und Uwe Vollmer (eds.)
Incentives and Economic Behaviour
Schriften zu Ordnungsfragen der Wirtschaft · Band 76 · Stuttgart · 2005

Law in Transition and Development: The Case of Russia

Dalia Marin

Contents

1. Introduction

Demonetization has become one of the dominant features of the Russian transition to a market economy. Different estimates suggest that the share of non-cash payments made 60 % of sales in 1998 in Russia and 50 % of sales in Ukraine in 1997.[1] The survey of 200 firms by the Russian Economic Barometer since 1992, in turn, suggests that non-cash payments rose steadily from 8 % in 1992 to 54 5 in mid-1998. Since the financial crisis in August of 1998 barter and other money surrogates have started to decline accounting for less than 10 % of receipts of industrial firms in February 2003. A similar picture emerges from a *Goskomstat* survey among 2000 large firms which reveals a share of non-cash payments of around 70 % in early 1998 and a subsequent decline to 60 % in 1999.

Figure 1:   Barter share of total transactions in Russia 1992 - 2003

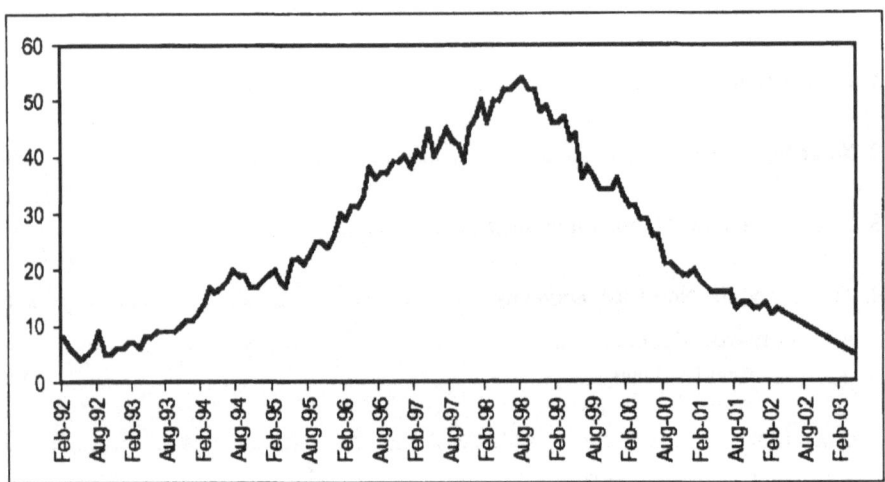

Source: *Russian Economic Barometer*

This time pattern of the process of demonetization is particularly puzzling. Barter started to rise after macroeconomic stabilization and has started to decline when macroeconomic instability set in after the August financial crisis. How can this time pattern of demonetization in the Russian economy be explained?

In this paper we look at the empirical validity of one of the most influential explanations of demonetization in Russia - the virtual economy argument.[2] The

---

[1] See *Commander* and *Mummsen* (1998) for Russia, *Marin, Kaufmann* and *Gorochowskij* (2000) for Ukraine.

[2] See *Gaddy* and *Ickes* (1998); for the empirical validity of other explanations, see *Marin, Kaufmann,* and *Gorochowskij* (2000).

argument claims that by allowing to change the prices of the goods exchanged in a hidden way barter helps different groups in the economy to keep the illusion that the manufacturing sector is producing valuable output while in fact it is not. Based on a unique deal-specific data set of 165 barter deals in Ukraine in 1997 we have information on the price differential between the cash and barter prices for the individual goods exchanged in barter deals. Thus, we can put the virtual economy argument to an empirical test. We find that illusion is not what is driving the actual pricing behavior in barter deals. We then proceed to offer a stylized model of how the observed pricing behavior in barter deals can be explained. The model sees the non-cash economy as an institutional response to the lack of trust and liquidity in the Russian economy. We test the price predictions of the model with actual price data and find that the data do not reject the trust view of the non-cash economy.

Why does it matter whether the "illusion-view" or the "trust-view" is better able to describe the actual development in Russia? The two views differ with respect to their policy implications of how to remonetize the Russian economy. If the "illusion-view" is correct, the main source of the problem lies in the real sector of the economy and barter is a "bad" thing because it allows the manufacturing sector to avoid restructuring and thus to avoid to get rid of the distortions in the real sector. If the "trust-view" is the correct description, then the main source of the problem lies in the financial sector of the economy and barter is a "good" thing because it allows the real sector to finance production when the banking sector does not fulfill its role of intermediation to channel private savings to finance investment in the real sector. According to both views barter helps to maintain production. The "illusion-view" sees barter to help maintain an inefficient output by pretending that it is valuable. The "trust-view" sees barter to help maintain a valuable output by overcoming a financial and input shortage which otherwise would lead to the collapse of output.

In a final section the paper concludes by discussing how a model based on trust can explain the evolution of barter over time in Russia and by discussing what has contributed to the vanishing barter economy after the August 1998 financial crisis in Russia.

By looking at how a model based on trust can explain the shift in the terms of trade of the non-cash economy in the former Soviet Union, this paper complements previous work on the subject. In *Marin* and *Schnitzer* (2003) we focus on the output decline in transition economies and we show how a model based on trust and liquidity can explain why the economic performance of the former Soviet Union was much worse than that of Central Europe. In *Marin, Kaufmann* and *Gorochowskij* (2000) we expose to the data several of the explanations of barter in transition economies which have been given in the literature like soft-budget constraints, market distortions, tax avoidance, and the lack of credit. Finally, in *Huang, Marin* and *Xu* (2003) we examine possible long-term costs of barter by focusing on the banking failure. We explore how barter may have contributed to a banking development trap which hinders the sector to fulfil its role as a financial institution in Russia.

2. Some Stylized Facts

We conducted a survey among 55 enterprises in Ukraine in 1997 from three cities Kyiv (50 %), Zaporioshje (30 %), and Dnipropetrovsk (20 %). From this survey we obtained deal-specific information on 165 barter deals. Each barter deal includes information on the selling firm and the buying firm and the type of goods exchanged. We distinguish the "sale" side of the barter deal and the "goods payment". The interviewed firms were selected from an address list of firms of the local office of the *Harvard Institute of International Development* in Kyiv. These firms were contacted by phone in order to secure their co-operation. The 55 firms of our sample were finally those who agreed to participate in the survey. The unit of analysis of the survey was one particular barter deal. Each firm provided us with information on three deals. The questionnaire asked for information on about forty dimensions on the "sale" and the "goods payment" side of the barter transaction. The "sale" was defined by the transaction of the seller who initiated the deal. The "goods payment" was the buyer's payment for the "sale". Because of the length of the questionnaire we personally visited these firms to fill in the questionnaire. Many of the firms were well informed about the firms they traded with because these firms served as financiers. This is how we obtained firm level information for about 100 firms (depending on the respective information) by interviewing 55 firms. The average share of barter in percent of firms' sales is 45 % with a minimum barter share of 1 % and a maximum share of 100 %. The barter deals are typically large in size ranging between US$ 10 and US$ 5,000,000 with a mean size of US$ 135,679. Firms' arrears make on average 30 % of firms' sales with a maximum of 626 %. On average, firms financed 6.31 % of output by bank debt with a maximum of over 100 %.

Table 1 identifies the type of firms involved in barter deals. The table illustrates that the non-cash economy is not an exclusive phenomenon of state owned enterprises. In 29.7 % of the deals the selling firm is a state enterprise and in 20.6 % a private firm. 4.2 % of the sample consist of barter deals with workers. On the buying end of the barter transaction the picture looks similar. In 29.5 % of the deals the buying firm is a state owned enterprise and in 25.2 % of the deals a private firm.[3]

Table 2 looks at the sectoral pattern of these 165 barter deals. Two things appear from the table. First, there is not much difference in the sectoral pattern between the "sale" side of the barter transaction and the "goods payment" side. Second, barter dominates in food and beverages, in the basic sector, and in machinery and vehicles.

---

[3] The firms in the address list were selected to secure representativity of the data material. Attention has been paid in particular to having a good representation of sectors, firm sizes, and ownership structure of firms compared to the Ukrainian economy. An ex post comparison of the data sample with available aggregate data indicates that the data are indeed fairly representative.

Table 1: **Ownership and the non-cash economy**

	selling firm in %	buying firm in %
domestic state or state controlled enterprise	29.70	29.45
domestic private firm	20.61	25.15
foreign firm	0.0	2.45
leaseholder / cooperative	1.82	4.29
worker	4.24	0.0
government	0.0	4.29
collective owned enterprise	33.94	29.45
GUS firm	4.24	4.29
joint-venture	5.45	0.61
total	100.00	100.00

Source: Survey of 165 barter deals in Ukraine in 1997.

Table 3 gives the terms of trade effect of the non-cash economy. From our survey data we have information on the percentage price difference between the barter price and the cash price for each of the 165 barter deals of the sample. We have this information for both sides - the "sale" and the "goods payment" of each deal so that we can calculate the net terms of trade effect of barter. SCASH is the percentage price difference between the barter price and the cash price on the "sale" side of the barter deal. PCASH is the percentage difference between the barter price and the cash price on the "goods payment" of the barter deal. TOT measures the net terms of trade of barter and is calculated by TOT = SCASH - PCASH.[4] It appears from the table that on the "sale" side of the deal the prices charged in barter are inflated by up to 50 % compared to cash deals. This happened in 23.3 % of the cases while in 73.6 % of the deals there was no difference between the two prices charged. In 3.1 % of the cases the firms involved discounted the price on the "sale" by up to 17 %.

In order to calculate who benefits from demonetization one has to look also at the pricing behavior on the "goods payment" side of the deal. Here it appears that in 25.9 % of the cases the firms discounted the price for the barter good compared to what they typically charge in cash deals by as much as 50 %. In 62.9 % of the deals there was no

---

[4] We obtained this information from the following question. "What is the percentage price difference between the price you charge/you are charged for this particular good in this barter deal as compared to the typical price you charge/you are charged for the same product in cash deals?"

Table 2:   **Sectoral pattern**

	"sale" in %	"goods payment" in %
natural resources	28.48	30.30
textile & leather	7.88	5.45
wood & paper	2.42	4.24
machinery & vehicles	16.97	23.03
food & beverages	16.36	22.42
chemicals	13.33	9.09
services	14.55	0.61
other	0.0	4.85
total	100.00	100.00

Source: Survey of 165 barter deals in Ukraine in 1997.

discounting or inflating on the barter prices for the goods payment. In 11.1 % of the deals the barter prices were inflated by as much as 200 %. Because of these differences in the pricing behavior between barter and cash deals, the net terms of trade effect of barter appears to be quite substantial ranging between -200 % and 50 %. As a result the non-cash economy appears to lead to a substantial shift in the terms of trade compared to the cash-economy. In almost 45 % of the deals barter shifts the terms of trade towards the "sale" side of the transaction. In those cases the "real" barter price of the "sale" is inflated by up to 50 % compared to the cash price for the same goods.

Table 3:   **Terms of trade**

differential between barter and cash price[1]					
"sale"		"goods payment"		"terms of trade"	
-17 % - 0 %	3.07	-50 % - 0 %	25.93	-200 % - 0 %	10.49
0 %	73.62	0 %	62.96	0 %	45.06
0 % - 50 %	23.31	0 % - 200 %	11.11	0 % - 50 %	44.44
total	100.00	total	100.00	total	100.00

[1] In % of cash price.
Source: Survey of 165 barter deals in Ukraine in 1997.

What explains this shift in the terms of trade of the non-cash economy? Why does barter lead to an increase of the real price for the "sale"? Who benefits from this shift and who loses? In the next two sections we look at two possible explanations for this shift in the terms of trade.

3. "Illusion" and the Non-Cash Economy

The virtual economy argument of *Gaddy* and *Ickes* (1998) rests on the assumption that the manufacturing sector does not produce valuable output and important groups in the economy (like the government and firms in different sectors) have an interest to pretend that this is not the case. According to this argument barter - a payment in goods or money surrogates rather than cash - is a way for these participants to keep the illusion of a value-creating manufacturing sector by allowing the latter sector to sell its output at a higher price than its market value and the value-adding natural resource sector to accept this overpricing out of lack of other opportunities. This way the manufacturing sector survives by drawing resources from the natural resource sector. According to the argument, keeping up the illusion of a value-adding manufacturing sector is highly costly for the Russian economy at large because this cross-subsidizing from the value-adding natural resource sector to the value-subtracting manufacturing sector prevents the manufacturing sector from moving into valuable activity. But if the natural resource sector is producing valuable output, why has the sector nothing better to do than to subsidize the manufacturing sector? In fact, the natural resource sector is supposed to have significant bargaining power in the interaction with other sectors when it is producing goods which the market values highly. Why then does the sector end up subsidizing the rest of the economy? The argument does not make much economic sense. However, the argument appeals to experts of central planning and policy observers in transition economies, because the practice of cross-subsidizing across different activities in the economy was a widespread feature of central planning. Therefore, let us pretend for a moment that the virtual economy argument does make economic sense and let us see whether it is actually true.

We can answer this question from our survey data, since we have information on the percentage price difference between the barter and cash prices for each of the 165 barter deals in the sample. We have this information for both sides (the "sale" and the "goods payment") of each barter deal so that we can calculate to whose favor the terms of trade shifts in non-cash transactions. As Table 3 illustrates the terms of trade shifts quite substantially in non-cash transactions. Thus, the virtual economy argument has the potential of explaining some of the variation in the terms of trade of barter.[5]

---

[5] The data are from Ukraine and not from Russia. Both countries are, however, very similar with respect the macroeconomic situation as well as the development of their legal and financial institutions.

If the virtual economy argument is valid, we expect that the manufacturing sector (like textiles, leather, machinery, and vehicles) is overpricing its output in barter compared to cash deals for the same product and pays less than the market value for natural resources (like electricity & gas). Furthermore, we expect this pricing distortion to be more pronounced for less efficient sectors.

In order to test these hypotheses we have to distinguish whether the sector is on the buying or selling end of the barter transaction. The reason is that overpricing the "sale" will benefit the sector which is on the selling end of the barter transaction and hurt the sector which is on the buying end of the same transaction. Similarly, discounting the price for the "goods payment" will benefit the sector which is on the buying end and hurt the sector which is on the selling end. TOT measures the net terms of trade and is calculated by TOT = SCASH - PCASH. Thus, when the sector is on the selling end and TOT takes a positive value, barter benefits this sector by shifting the terms of trade in its favor. Similarly, when the sector is on the buying end and TOT takes a positive value, then barter hurts this sector by shifting the terms of trade in its disfavor.

We are now ready to put the virtual economy argument to an empirical test. Table 4 examines whether differences in the pricing behavior across sectors can be identified. The table aggregates the 165 barter deals into 4 sectors and looks at their pricing behavior in non-cash deals compared to cash deals. The table distinguishes whether the sector is on the selling or buying end of the transaction. From Table 4 it appears that there is no systematic difference in the pricing behavior across sectors in non-cash transactions (the *F-test* of the *Analysis of Variance (Anova)* is not statistically significant at conventional levels). Take the example of the manufacturing sector which includes textiles, leather, machinery and vehicles, and chemicals. When this sector is on the selling end of the transaction, it overprices its output on average by 4.03 % compared to cash deals and it is discounted on the goods payment by 0.75 % on average, so that the sector's net benefit from barter is 4.78 % (in terms of its cash price).[6] So far so good. But the same appears to be true for the natural resource sector which includes electricity and gas, coke, petroleum, metal ores and non-metallic minerals. This sector's net benefit from barter is 4.88 % (in terms of its cash price). What seems to matter here for the pricing behavior in non-cash transactions is not the sector, but whether the sector is on the selling or buying end of the transaction. Take again the example of the manufacturing sector. When this sector is on the buying end of the barter deal, it pays more for the "sale" by 4.81 % on average and sells its "good payment" at a 3.52 % discount compared to cash deals, so that the sector's net loss from barter is 8.33 % on average. This net loss from non-cash transactions appears to be happening in all the other sectors as well, when the sector is a buyer rather than a seller.

---

[6] The average percent price differential between barter and cash appear to be low from Table 4. These averages hide the actual variation in the price differentials, because in 45 % of the deals the non-cash and cash prices were equal. For the distribution of the price differentials see Table 3.

Table 4: **Pricing behavior of sectors**

		selling sector			buying sector		
		SCASH[1]	PCASH[2]	TOT[3]	SCASH	PCASH	TOT
electricity & gas	mean	0.00	-4.12	4.12	3.78	7.42	-3.64
	std. dev.	0.00	8.52	8.52	8.80	45.06	42.11
	N	17	17	17	18	18	18
coke & petroleum	mean	5.48	1.45	4.03	1.13	-1.31	2.44
	std. dev.	14.45	10.28	8.37	5.50	6.54	6.57
	N	13	13	13	16	16	16
metal ores & other non- metallic minerals	mean	5.00	-1.29	6.29	2.50	0.58	1.92
	std. dev.	10.16	6.05	10.05	8.09	17.02	18.29
	N	17	17	17	18	18	18
food & beverages	mean	2.64	1.00	1.64	3.03	-2.47	5.51
	std. dev.	6.53	38.45	35.75	9.45	15.38	14.09
	N	27	27	27	36	36	36
textiles & leather	mean	1.86	0.26	1.61	5.21	-4.17	9.38
	std. dev.	8.46	6.86	9.99	7.11	7.93	9.66
	N	16	16	16	12	12	12
machinery & verhicles	mean	3.66	0.91	2.75	3.46	-5.06	8.52
	std. dev.	7.41	10.64	13.51	7.67	9.96	11.40
	N	28	28	28	30	30	30
chemicals	mean	6.08	-3.60	9.68	7.19	0.07	7.12
	std. dev.	9.49	12.50	11.18	9.47	12.01	8.59
	N	22	22	22	15	15	15
services	mean	2.83	-4.04	6.86	0.00	-10.00	10.00
	std. dev.	6.54	17.72	16.27	-	-	-
	N	23	23	23	1	1	1
total	mean	3.43	-1.16	4.59	3.52	-1.21	4.73
	std. dev.	8.30	18.63	18.07	8.26	19.66	18.86
	N	163	163	163	146	146	146
Anova	F-test	1.08	0.33	0.52	0.76	0.77	0.93
	sign. level	(0.382)	(0.937)	(0.817)	(0.619)	(0.614)	(0.489)

[1] Difference between the barter price and the cash price in percent of the cash price in the "sale" side of the barter deal.

[2] Difference between the barter price and the cash price in percent of the cash price in the "goods payment" of the barter deal.

[3] TOT = SCASH - PCASH.

It appears then that the sectors gain from barter when they sell and they loose from barter when they buy. This is not what we would have expected if we believed in the virtual economy argument of Russia's non-cash economy.

We now examine whether this result depends on the level of aggregation of sectors. In Table 5 we aggregate the sectors to a natural resource sector (including electricity and gas, coke and petroleum, metal ores and other non-metallic minerals) and to a manufacturing sector (including textiles, leather, machinery, vehicles, and chemicals). We construct a variable which we call *virtual economy 1* which includes all deals in which the natural resource sector was on the selling end of the transaction and the manufacturing sector on the buying end. If the virtual economy argument is valid then we expect to see a discount on the "sale" price and a mark-up over the cash price on the "goods payment" leading to a net terms of trade shift in favor of the manufacturing sector. A look at Table 5 reveals that the opposite is the case. The natural resource sector lives at the expense of the manufacturing sector who suffers a loss in the terms of trade of 6.88 % on average when the natural resource sector is the seller and manufacturing the buyer in the transaction. Can the manufacturing sector draw on the resources of the natural resource sector when he is selling to this sector rather than buying from it? This case is captured by the variable *virtual economy 2* which includes all deals in which manufacturing is the seller and the natural resources sector the buyer in the transaction. The table reveals that in this case both sectors are overpricing their output in non-cash transactions compared to cash leading to a slight terms of trade gain for the manufacturing sector of 1.13 %. Moreover, the constellation of the manufacturing sector as the seller and the natural resource sector as the buyer in barter has been taking place in 23 deals only out of a total of 165 deals. These numbers are much too small to plausibly explain the enormous shift towards non-cash transactions in Russia. Furthermore, the F-tests reject the hypothesis that there is any difference in the pricing behavior for both constellations.

We turn now to the second prediction of the virtual economy argument. The bottom part of Table 5 examines whether the price distortions between non-cash and cash deals are more pronounced for less efficient firms. If the virtual economy argument is valid we expect this to be the case, because firms with lower productivity will need to inflate their prices by more or get bigger discounts for the barter goods in order to pretend to produce value added. From the table it appears that there is no statistical significant relation between the price distortions and the efficiency of the firm. If at all, it appears to be the firms with productivity levels in the middle range who show the largest price differentials between non-cash and cash transactions.[7]

In Table 6 we look at the distribution of the terms of trade of barter for two leading sectors: manufacturing and electricity & gas. The first three columns of the table give the pricing behavior of electricity & gas when the sector is on the selling end of the transaction. It can be seen from the table that the sector charges the same price as in cash deals when it sells electricity & gas and receives in more than 20 % of the deals a discount of up to 50 % for the goods he is paid with so that the terms of trade shifts in

---

[7]   Moreover, *Marin, Kaufmann* and *Gorochowskij* (2000) show that the firm's barter exposure does not increase for less efficient firms.

Table 5:   **Is Russia's economy virtual?**

	% price differential on						N
	"sale"[1]		"goods payment"[2]		"terms of trade"[3]		
	mean	std. dev.	mean	std. dev.	mean	std. dev.	
virtual economy 1							
seller: natural resources[4]							
buyer: manufacturing[5]	1.47	4.24	-5.41	9.24	6.88	9.30	17
other	3.66	8.63	-0.66	19.39	4.32	18.84	146
total	3.43	8.30	-1.16	18.63	4.59	18.07	163
Anova F-Test		1.06		0.99		0.31	
sign. level		(0.306)		(0.321)		(0.581)	
virtual economy 2							
seller: manufacturing[5]							
buyer: natural resources[4]	1.43	5.85	0.30	12.91	1.13	14.20	23
other	3.76	8.61	-1.40	19.44	5.15	18.62	140
total	3.43	8.30	-1.16	18.63	4.59	18.07	163
Anova F-Test		1.55		0.16		0.98	
sign. level		(0.215)		(0.686)		(0.324)	
firm's efficiency[6]							
low	3.13	7.78	-0.13	11.21	3.27	12.26	57
medium	2.76	7.07	-4.88	10.60	7.64	12.24	60
high	2.91	10.11	1.16	33.96	1.75	31.29	36
total	2.93	8.08	-1.69	19.03	4.62	18.58	153
Anova F-Test		0.03		1.45		1.38	
sign. level		(0.969)		(0.239)		(0.255)	

[1] Difference between the barter price and the cash price in percent of the cash price in the "sale" side of the barter deal, denoted SCASH.

[2] Difference between the barter price and the cash price in percent of the cash price in the "goods payment" of the barter deal, denoted PCASH.

[3] Terms of trade = SCASH - PCASH.

[4] Includes electricity & gas, coke & petroleum and metal ores & other non-metallic minerals.

[5] Includes textiles & leather, machinery & vehicles, and chemicals.

[6] Output per employee. Low: 1,000 to 7,500 US$, medium: 7,100 to 15,000 US$, high: 15,100 to 140,000 US$.

more than 20 % of the deals in favor of the electricity & gas sector. The table shows no single case in which this sector has been subsidizing an other sector when doing a barter deal. The next three columns of the table look at the pricing behavior of electricity & gas when this sector is on the buying end of the transaction. In this case the sector buys in more than 16 % of the deals an overpriced good from other sectors (the price is inflated by up to 50 %) and gives a discount on electricity & gas of up to 50 % when selling it to other sectors so that the sector ends up with a terms of trade loss of up to 50 % in 33 % of the deals. When this terms of trade loss of the electricity & gas sector is compared to the terms of trade loss of the manufacturing sector as a buyer (as can be seen in the last column of the same table) the latter sector has to suffer a loss in 53.6 % of the deals (compared to 33 % of electricity & gas).

Table 6:   **Terms of trade** (in %)

	seller gas & electricity			buyer gas & electricity		
	SCASH	PCASH	TOT	SCASH	PCASH	TOT
< 0 %	0.0	23.53	0.0	0.0	22.22	5.56
0 %	100.00	76.47	76.47	83.33	72.22	61.11
> 0 %	0.0	0.0	23.53	16.67	5.56	33.33
missing	0.0	0.0	0.0	0.0	0.0	0.0
total	100.00	100.00	100.00	100.00	100.00	100.00
	seller manufacturing[1]			buyer manufacturing[1]		
	SCASH	PCASH	TOT	SCASH	PCASH	TOT
< 0 %	4.48	20.90	10.45	1.45	26.09	5.80
0 %	62.69	68.66	40.30	66.67	63.77	39.13
> 0 %	31.34	8.96	47.76	31.88	8.70	53.62
missing	1.49	1.49	1.49	0.0	1.45	1.45
total	100.00	100.00	100.00	100.00	100.00	100.00

[1] Manufacturing: textiles & leather, wood & paper, machinery & vehicles, and chemicals.
Source: Survey of 165 barter deals in Ukraine in 1997.

To conclude, the virtual economy argument is virtual and has no basis in the data. Who benefits from the non-cash economy does not depend on the sector, as the argument claims, but is exclusively driven by the selling or buying status of firms. But why would the selling or buying status of firms determine in who's favor the terms of trade shifts in barter? Or to put it differently, why are frequently prices for the "sale" inflated and prices for the "goods payment" discounted in barter transactions? We turn to an answer to this question in the next section.[8]

4. "Trust" and the Non-Cash Economy

If the virtual economy argument has no empirical basis, how can we explain that the seller is overpricing the "sale" and the buyer is discounting the price for the "goods payment" in non-cash transactions? If hiding a valueless output is not the reason, what else motivates such pricing behavior? We turn now to a model for an answer.

4.1. A Stylized Model[9]

Consider a good which requires n steps of production to become a final good. Each production step is carried out by a different firm. After n steps of refinement the intermediate good becomes a final good. Each buyer along the chain can negotiate only with his supplier. This leads to n bargaining problems along the chain. At each of these steps we assume *Nash* bargaining with both parties equally sharing the joint surplus. The value of the surplus is denoted by $v > 0$. Intermediate goods are assumed to have zero value when sold outside the production chain.

Lets looks at the first production chain in more detail. Consider a supplier of the original input good, S_l, and the buyer B_l. We assume that B_l makes a relationship specific investment i at date 0.9. This investment can be thought of as the time and money B_l spends in order to find an adequate supplier. At the time of this investment, the two firms are assumed not to be able to write a contract which commits S_l to deliver the input good for a particular price in the future. Thus, B_l must first invest and only then – when the investment costs are sunk – can bargain over the input price. This leads to a hold-up problem in the bargaining of the price when the input good is actually delivered.

At date 1, the two parties can negotiate about the delivery of S_l's input good and about the price. v_l denotes the value of the input good to B_l. We assume that B_l cannot pay cash at the time of delivery of the input good because he is liquidity constraint. Thus, S_l has to deliver the input good on a credit basis, if at all. B_l will be able to pay when he is paid v_l by the next firm in the production chain. We assume that enforcing credit repayment to be difficult in transition economies and thus S_l has to incur some

---

[8] The fact that the terms of trade is shifting in 45 % of the deals towards the "sale" side of the barter deal casts further doubts on the explanation that barter is driven by tax motives. As Table 3 shows it is only in 10.5 % of the deals in which firms could potentially hide some of their profits lowering their tax base. This number corresponds roughly to the number of cases in which the interviewed firms gave taxes some importance for undertaking a barter deal, see *Marin, Kaufmann* and *Gorochowskij* (2000).

[9] This section follows *Marin* and *Schnitzer* (2003).

fixed cost x to enforce repayment of p_l. This cost could be thought of as the cost of using the courts and lawyers fees and potential bribes for judges or other public officials or the cost of private enforcement like the use of Mafia etc.[10]

At date 1.1 after delivery of the input good B_l can try to default on some of his payment. Let $\tilde{p}_1$ denote the price paid by B_l at this date. Figure 2 summarizes the time sequence of the bargaining at production step 1.

Figure 2:   Bargaining at the production step 1

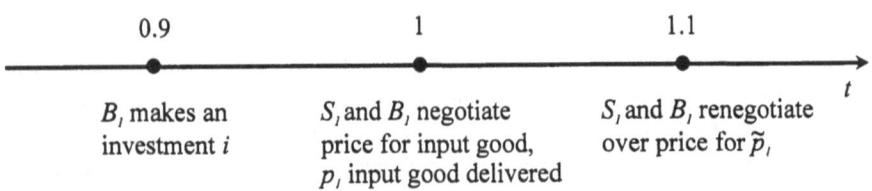

Let us solve production step 1 recursively. Recall that at date 1, when S_l delivers the input good, B_l has no cash to pay for the input. Thus, once the input supplier delivers the input, the bargaining power reverses and shifts to B_l. Now the input supplier has to worry of being paid. At date 1.1, after realizing his profits from selling the input to the next firm, B_l has enough cash to pay but if he does not do so voluntarily S_l has to incur cost x to enforce payment of p_l. Suppose B_l holds up now the input supplier and refuses to pay the full price p_l on which the two parties agreed at date 1, but offers to pay $\tilde{p}_1 = p_1 - x$ instead. If this happens, S_l can either accept this payment or enforce p_l at cost x. In equilibrium he will accept B_l's reduced payment.

At date 1, the two parties have to agree on a price p_l. Since B_l's investment i is already sunk at this date, it is not taken into account in the bargaining over the input price. Thus, B_l might not invest in finding a supplier relationship because these costs are not covered by the price. This is what constitutes the hold up problem of buyer B_l. However, the two parties anticipate at date 1 that B_l will exploit his position after delivery of the input good and pay a reduced price at date 1.1. Assuming *Nash* bargaining whenever possible this implies that a price p_l is chosen such that

---

[10] The literature on contract enforcement in Eastern Europe suggests that enforcement with the help of legal institutions is possible but costly, see *Hendley, Murrell* and *Ryterman* (1999); *Johnson, McMillan* and *Woodruff* (1999) get a similar result from their survey among five transition countries that legal institutions do matter and are used although relational contracting dominates.

(1)
$$v_1 - \left(p_1 - x\right) = p_1 - x \leftrightarrow p_1 = \frac{v_1}{2} + x,$$

i.e., in anticipation of B_I's future price reduction, S_I marks up p_I in the first place, if this is possible.

However, inflating the input price in anticipation of the price reduction at date 1.1 will not always be possible. B_I's liquidity constraint - the cash he gets when he himself sells the good to the next buyer, i.e. v_I - puts an upper bound on the maximum payment that can be enforced at cost x. Thus, in order to fully capture the subsequent price reduction S_I may want to inflate the price by more than can credibly be enforced as payment at date 1.1, since even at cost x, B_I cannot be forced to pay more than he has in his pockets at date 1.1. Thus,

(2)
$$p_1 = \min\left(\frac{v_1}{2} + x; v_1\right).$$

If x is sufficiently large, i.e. $x > v_I/2$, B_I's liquidity constraint becomes binding which will make it impossible for S_I to pass on these costs to him. B_I's cash from the sale to the next firm will simply not be enough to fully cover these costs. In this case, B_I can exploit the fact that he is liquidity constrained to prevent to be held up by the input supplier. This will, however, only work when enforcement costs x are just right. When x is low, i.e. $x < v_I/2$, then S_I is able to pass on x in the price mark-up. In this case, the buyer's liquidity constraint does not prevent an equal sharing of the surplus. When x becomes too large, i.e. $x > v_I$, then B_I captures the entire surplus and S_I cannot guarantee himself a positive payoff. Thus, in order for the liquidity constraint to alleviate B_I's hold-up problem we have

(3)
$$\frac{v_1}{2} < i \leq x < v_1.$$

Without a liquidity constraint and enforcement costs, B_I's payoff would be $v_I/2$, i.e. half the value of production at the first production step, and if $i > v_I/2$ then no production would take place at all, because the surplus does not cover B_I's investment costs i. However, if enforcement costs are sufficiently high, B_I can exploit this fact to capture more than one half of the production value. Thus, B_I's ex post bargaining power has to be sufficiently large to cover his ex ante investment, i.e. $i \leq x$ in order for production to take place. Since S_I needs a positive profit in order to participate in the deal, enforcement costs may not be too high either; i.e. $x < v_I$.

We have just seen that S_I may not be willing to deliver the input good if the credit problem is too severe, i.e. if $x > v_I$. Thus, if the buyer has no cash and the legal system to enforce payment is poorly developed a potentially valuable transaction does not take place. Can barter – a trade credit in goods rather than cash – help under these circumstances?

Suppose B_I can produce one unit of a barter good, but only after date 1. Let w denote the value of the barter good and let k denote B_I's production cost. If B_I sells this barter good to someone outside the production chain he does so at a cash price $p^c = (w+k)/2$, assuming again *Nash* bargaining. This would give B_I a payoff of $(w - k)/2$. However, B_I can also use this barter good as a collateral to improve his creditworthiness. In this case, B_I promises to deliver the barter good to S_I when credit repayment is due. The price for this barter good, p^B, is fixed together with p_I before S_I decides about his input delivery. The two parties negotiate prices p_I and p^B such that they split the surplus of both transactions equally, taking into account the renegotiation on p_I at date 1.1. This means that the inclusion of the barter trade allows B_I to shift some profit back to S_I by discounting the price of the barter good p^B. Note, however, that p^B cannot be chosen arbitrarily small because B_I cannot be forced to deliver the barter good as promised, but has to be induced to do so voluntarily. If B_I cheats on S_I and refuses to deliver, all S_I can do, given that B_I has signed a contract that promises delivery of the barter good, is to try to prevent a sale of the barter good to someone else. We assume that S_I suceeds with such an attempt with probability $(1-\pi)$ which reduces B_I's potential payoff from selling the barter good to $\pi(w-k)/2$, where $\pi < 1$. This effectively means that barter creates a hostage of a given size z, where

$$(4) \qquad z = (1-\pi)\frac{(w-k)}{2}.$$

Note first, that the size of the hostage z created by barter depends on two things. First, the value of the hostage increases with the value of the good offered as a means of payment in barter. This is given by the payoff $(w-k)/2$ when the good is sold independently of barter. Second, the value of the hostage declines with B_I's cheating payoff when he defaults on payment which is expressed by $\pi(w-k)/2$. The difference between these two payoffs is determined by the parameter π and captures the commitment value which B_I achieves by agreeing to repay the trade credit in goods rather than cash. By doing so, B_I reduces his chances to sell the barter good to someone else than S_I. $(1-\pi)$ is the probability of being caught when B_I cheats on repayment and sells the barter good to someone else than S_I. The parameter π can be thought of as a measure of how well the input seller can label the barter good as his property. The smaller π, the less "anonymous" the means of payment and the smaller B_I's cheating surplus from defaulting on payment. Thus, the smaller π, the larger the commitment value of barter and the larger the hostage z. B_I uses the barter contract as a commitment not to exploit his bargaining power and to shift some profit back to S_I in order to make him participate in the deal when his profit from the input transaction is too low due to large credit enforcement cost x. In this sense, barter creates a deal-specific collateral that helps to alleviate the hold-up problem when credit enforcement is prohibitively costly.[11]

What does the model imply for the pricing behavior in barter transactions? We need to evaluate how the hold-up problem and the credit problem just described will be reflected in the terms of the barter contract. We have just argued that the hold-up problem in the input deal can be alleviated if the input buyer faces a credit constraint and barter is used if credit enforcement becomes too costly for the input seller. Thus, we expect this problems to be reflected in the prices chosen in non-cash transactions as compared to prices in cash deals where no such problems are present.

Recall from equation (2) that the price for the input good in barter is

$$(5) \qquad p_1 = \min\left(\frac{v_1}{2} + x; v_1\right).$$

Compare this price with the cash price for the same input with no such problems. Without the hold-up problem the price for the input will reflect the fact that B_I has undertaken an investment, because in this case the investment cost i can be contracted on before B_I's investment takes place. Furthermore, the input price will not reflect the credit enforcement cost x, because in this case B_I has no liquidity constraint and thus there are no enforcement costs x. Splitting the surplus implies a cash price

---

[11] *Kranton* (1996) suggests that barter as a form of reciprocal exchange can be quite costly by locking trading partner in.

(6)
$$p_1^c = \frac{(v_1 - i)}{2}.$$

Comparing (5) and (6) shows that within barter the price for the "sale" side of the deal will be inflated compared to the cash price for the same input, because the cash price will take into account B_1's investment cost i (because there is no hold-up problem) and will not include a mark-up for the credit enforcement cost x (because there is no credit problem).

If p_1 cannot be increased anymore because it reaches its upper bound v_1, then we expect the price for the "goods payment" to be discounted. When the liquidity constraint is binding and thus S_1 cannot inflate the price for the "sale", barter allows B_1 to shift some of the profit back to S_1 by giving a discount on the "goods payment". Thus, we expect that the hold-up problem and the credit problem both shift the terms of trade in favor of the input supplier, either by an increase of p_1 as compared to p_1^c or when this is not possible by a decrease of p^B as compared to the cash price for the barter good or both.

4.2. Empirical Evidence

We are now ready to put the model to an empirical test to see whether the incentive problems just described can indeed explain some of the observed pricing behavior in non-cash transactions.

For the regression analysis we will use SCASH, PCASH, and TOT as the indepentent variables. Recall that TOT is defined as the difference of SCASH and PCASH, where SCASH and PCASH are the percentage differences between the barter price and the cash price for the input good (the "sale") and the barter good (the "goods payment"), respectively. First, we have to find proxies for the incentive problems described in the previous section. We measure the severety of the hold up problem on the input good by the complexity index suggested by Blanchard and Kremer (1997). We construct a deal-specific complexity measure for the input good SCOMPLEX. SCOMPLEX is an index that takes the value of zero if the "sale" is produced with one input only and approaches one when the "sale" good uses several inputs from other sectors. The number of inputs required for the "sale" good to be produced stands here for the number of bargaining problems B_1 faces. We matched the ISIC sectors of the "sale" good with the sector of the complexity index given by Blanchard and Kremer (1997). We use as a measure for the credit problem (a measure for x) the input buyer's B_1 outstanding firm arrears PARREARS. The idea is that the more B_1 is indebted already the less likely it is that he will repay the trade credit and thus the lower his creditworthiness.

Table 7 shows the regressions explaining SCASH, PCASH, and TOT with these two incentive problems. The more complex the "sale" good the more severe is the hold-up problem in the input deal and thus the larger the barter price p_1 relative to the cash price p_1^c. Thus, we expect a positive sign on the complexity variable SCOMPLEX in the SCASH regressions (given in columns 1 - 5 of the table).[12] We have no prediction for SCOMPLEX in the PCASH regressions (given in columns 6 - 10 of the table). Because of the positive effect of SCOMPLEX on SCASH we expect also a positive sign for SCOMPLEX in the TOT regressions (given in columns 11 - 15). This is supported by the results of the table. The input specific complexity measure is positive and significant in all the SCASH and TOT regressions. Thus, the "real" prices for the "sale" appears to be inflated because of the presence of a hold-up problem in the input deal.

Turning to the credit problem we expect PARREARS to have a positive effect on SCASH, since S_1 will inflate the barter price for the input p_1 relative to the cash price p_1^c to cover the anticipated credit enforcement costs x. Furthermore, we expect a negative sign for the PARREARS variable in the regressions for PCASH, since barter is undertaken to shift some of the profit back to the supplier by discounting the price for the barter good. Because of these effects on barter prices on both sides of the transaction, we expect PARREARS to have a positive effect on TOT. Turning to the results, we see that PARREARS is insignificant in the SCASH regressions which suggests that the supplier is not able to pass on the credit enforcement costs to the buyer. PARREARS turns out to be highly significant and negative in the PCASH regressions. These results for the PARREARS variable in the SCASH and PCASH regressions support the story given by the model of the previous section. Barter is needed to save the deal exactly when the supplier is unable to pass on the enforcement costs to the buyer and as a result does not expect to have a positive profit from the transaction. Discounting the price for the barter good is then a way to make the deal go through by shifting back part of the profit to the supplier. This explains why the prices for the "goods payment" are predominantly discounted compared to cash prices for the same goods.

Finally, we include several sectoral dummies (SMANUF, PMANUF, SRECOURCES, PRESOURCES, VIRTUAL 1, VIRTUAL 2) to test whether those have any explanatory power for the pricing behavior in non-cash transactions. None of these variables are significant at conventional levels except for the variable SMANUF in the PCASH and TOT regressions. The positive and significant sign of the estimated coefficient for SMANUF in the PCASH regressions and its negative and significant effect in the TOT regressions suggests, however, that the manufacturing sector suffers losses in the terms of trade by being overpriced on the "goods payment" even when the sector is a seller in barter transactions. Thus, the manufacturing sector is the only sector that appears to never gain from non-cash transactions. This is just the opposite of what the virtual economy argument suggests. Note that this finding of the regression analysis

---

[12] Note that the estimated coefficient on the complexity index can be used to test whether the hold-up problem is on the buyer's or on the seller's side. A positive coefficient indicates that the buyer is held-up by the seller rather than the other way around.

Table 7: Terms of trade of non-cash transactions

	SCASH					PCASH					TOT				
	(1)	(2)	(3)	(4)	(5)	(6)	(7)	(8)	(9)	(10)	(11)	(12)	(13)	(14)	(15)
SCOMPLEX	0.206	0.196	0.201	0.196	0.201	-0.110	-0.081	-0.107	-0.081	-0.108	0.316	0.277	0.308	0.277	0.308
	(0.020)	(0.031)	(0.026)	(0.032)	(0.027)	(0.160)	(0.282)	(0.181)	(0.284)	(0.183)	(0.004)	(0.010)	(0.006)	(0.011)	(0.006)
PARREARS	0.004	0.004	0.003	0.005	0.003	-0.024	-0.026	-0.024	-0.025	-0.024	0.028	0.030	0.027	0.030	0.027
	(0.599)	(0.548)	(0.689)	(0.476)	(0.691)	(0.000)	(0.000)	(0.001)	(0.000)	(0.001)	(0.002)	(0.001)	(0.004)	(0.001)	(0.004)
SRESOURCES		-1.432		-0.749			2.097		2.842			-3.529		-3.591	
		(0.523)		(0.769)			(0.271)		(0.189)			(0.186)		(0.237)	
SMANUF		-0.697		-0.744			6.248		6.196			-6.944		-6.940	
		(0.792)		(0.779)			(0.007)		(0.007)			(0.029)		(0.031)	
PRESOURCES			-1.155		-0.542			-0.387		-0.997			-0.769		0.455
			(0.644)		(0.845)			(0.864)		(0.689)			(0.802)		(0.893)
PMANUF			0.273		0.273			-0.502		-0.502			0.775		0.775
			(0.901)		(0.902)			(0.800)		(0.801)			(0.774)		(0.774)
VIRTUAL 1				-1.553					-1.696					0.142	
				(0.566)					(0.458)					(0.965)	
VIRTUAL 2					-2.299					2.288					-4.587
					(0.597)					(0.559)					(0.389)
R^2adj.	0.058	0.034	0.033	0.023	0.021	0.185	0.259	0.159	0.254	0.149	0.210	0.246	0.187	0.234	0.184
N	64	64	64	64	64	64	64	64	64	64	64	64	64	64	64

P-values in paranthesis.
Source: Survey of 165 barter deals in Ukraine in 1997.

is somewhat not consistent with the results in Table 4 of section 3 in which the manufacturing sector as a seller gains from barter. A closer look at Table 4 reveals, however, that the manufacturing sector like textiles, leather, machinery, vehicles is gaining the least as a seller in barter transactions compared to the rest of the economy. For example, the sectors textiles and leather are gaining 1.6 % on average as a seller compared to a gain of 6.3 % of metal ores and of 4.6 % when all selling sectors are aggregated (given in the bottom of Table 4). These averages hide the distribution of the mark-ups on the "sale" which the regression analysis takes into account. This is the reason why Table 4 gives a small gain for manufacturing as a selling sector while the regression analysis indicates a loss from barter for this case.

5. Conclusion

In this paper we explore an influential explanation for the non-cash economy in Russia, the virtual economy argument, based on deal-specific price data of 165 barter deals in Ukraine. We find that the argument is not consistent with the actual pricing behavior in barter deals. First, there appears to be no statistically significant difference in the pricing behavior across sectors. Second, the only sector which appears to suffer a loss from the non-cash economy is the manufacturing sector.

We then proceed to offer a model based on the lack of trust and liquidity. The pricing predictions from this model are then put to an empirical test. It turns out that real prices on the "sale" side of the barter transaction are inflated, because they reflect a trust problem and a credit problem between input suppliers and producing firms. Input suppliers are exploiting the fact that there are only a few suppliers around and thus switching suppliers is costly and charge higher prices for their inputs in barter deals compared to cash deals (this is how the trust problem materializes). If this price mark-up for inputs would happen in cash deals firms would refuse to buy those expensive inputs and prefer not to produce. Furthermore, input suppliers have to incur costs of enforcing payment (they have to involve the Mafia or legal firms) which they want to be covered by the deal. If these credit enforcement costs become very large (which happens when legal institutions do not work properly or when firms are already very indebted) then input suppliers will refuse to deliver the inputs in cash deals because they cannot expect a positive profit. Thus, in a cash economy the lack of trust and liquidity prevent many profitable trades from taking place.

In a non-cash economy the deal can go through by choosing the "right" prices for the "sale" and the "goods payment", because of two reasons. First, by introducing a second profitable transaction in the form of the "goods payment" the producing firm can buy an inflated input and still make a profit.[13] Second, the input supplying firm gets a discount

---

[13] The model actually predicts that in equilibrium the hold-up problem is "solved" and thus input prices will not be inflated. A look at Table 3 reveals that in 73.6 % of the deals this was actually the case.

on the barter good which allows her to cover the credit enforcement cost. Thus, the non-cash economy helps to maintain output which otherwise would collapse due to imperfect input and credit markets. The imperfections of input and credit markets are reflected in a shift in the terms of trade of barter. Through the inflated price for the "sale" and the price discount on the "goods payment" the deal is actually saved by guarantying both parties a positive profit. The shift in the terms of trade is the mechanism by which the non-cash economy accomplishes to maintain output which otherwise would collapse in a cash economy.

5.1. The Time Pattern of Barter

How can this story explain the time pattern of demonetization in Russia given in Figure 1? In 1992 firms have accumulated substantial debt among each other due to a refusal of the banking sector to provide credit. Firms turned to other firms for trade credits when bank credit was not available. Accumulated arrears reached a critical level in 1995 at which production was unsustainable due to prohibitively large credit enforcement costs. At this point firms refused to extend further trade credit (in cash) to each other out of the worry of not being paid. Barter then stepped in as the only way to maintain production. At this point barter started to substitute for the non active banking sector as well as for trade credits in cash which explains the explosive increase. Why then has barter started to decline with the financial crisis in 1998?

In order to get to an answer it is useful to compare Russia with Ukraine. Both countries are similar with respect to the time patter of barter (in both countries barter exploded until 1998 and declined thereafter), but they differ with respect to the exchange rate and oil ressources. Russia is an oil exporter, Ukraine is an oil importer. The *ruble* depreciated by about 50 % after the August financial crisis, while the *hryvnia* showed only a modest decline. The strong devaluation of the exchange rate and booming world oil markets have both been argued to have contributed to the vanishing barter economy after 1998.[14] However, the different behavior of the exchange rates and the difference in the importance of oil in these two countries suggests that some other force must be at work to explain the striking similarity in the time pattern of barter.

Is the virtual economy argument a candidate explanation? To construct an argument for the vanishing barter economy along the lines of the virtual economy hypothesis one has to find a reason why in 1998 the energy producers stopped providing subsidies to the manufacturing sector. Is it because the energy producers had less money available? Or because manufacturing firms suddenly started to create value in 1998? The booming world oil markets and the associated increase in rents of the energy sector should have made it easier rather than more difficult for this sector to transfer value to the rest of the economy. Why then has barter started to decline in 1998? The virtual economy argument does not seem to offer an answer.

---

[14] See *Ahrend, Aukutsionek* and *Parilova* (2000) and *OECD* (2000) who make a similar point.

5.2. Out of a Banking Development Trap?

In order to find an answer for the decline in barter we have to turn to the financial sector. One common feature between Ukraine and Russia that the virtual economy argument does not touch upon is the financial sector. Russia and Ukraine are the transition countries with the lowest level of bank intermediation (see *Huang, Marin, and Xu* 2003). Banks practically did not lend to the real sector and financed the government budget instead. *Huang, Marin,* and *Xu* (2003) argue that this was due to a banking development trap. Banks are not able to distinguish good credit risk firms from bad ones. They charge interest rates that cover the average credit risk of all borrowing firms. This, in turn, induces low credit-risk firms to turn to barter trade to avoid subsidizing the high credit risk firms. The option for low credit-risk firms to raise liquidity through barter trade drives up bank lending rates, since banks expect higher credit-risk firms to remain in the pool of borrowing firms. In equilibrium, only high credit-risk firms borrow from banks while the low credit-risk firms turn to barter. The banking sector looks for high yield government securities in which to invest. The financial sector is separated from the real sector of the economy which hinders banking sector development.

With the collapse of the treasury bills market after the August financial crisis banks lending behavior changed drastically. They stopped to finance the government budget and have started to lend to firms. The vanished market for government bonds induced the banks to reallocate their assets to the real sector of the economy. They lowered interest rates to attract borrowers. Lower interest rates made it attractive for some better risk firms to start borrowing from banks rather than to continue to barter trade. This improved the creditworthiness of the pool of borrowers and, in turn, further lowered interest rates and induced more firms to switch from barter to bank loans. This way, the financial crisis of 1998 helped Russia and Ukraine to get out of a banking development trap which explains why barter has dropped (see *Huang, Marin* and *Xu* 2003).

References

Ahrend, Rudiger; Sergei Aukutsionek and *Sveta Parilova* (2000), Russian Industry - Cashless or Hopeless? - Explaining a Decade of Barter, Russian European Centre for Economic Policy, Moscow.

Blanchard, Olivier and *Michael Kremer* (1997), Disorganization, in: Quarterly Journal of Economics, Vol. 112, pp. 1091-1126.

Calvo, Guillermo A. and *Fabrizio Coricelli* (1995a), Inter-enterprise Arrears in Economies in Transition, in: *Holzmann, Robert* et al. (eds.): Output Decline in Eastern Europe, Dordrecht, pp. 193-212.

Calvo, Guillermo A. and *Fabrizio Coricelli* (1995b), Output Collapse in Eastern Europe: The Role of Credit, in: *Blejer, Mario I.; Guillermo Calvo; Fabrizio Coricelli* and *Andrew*

Gelb (eds.): Eastern Europe in Transition: From Recession to Growth?, World Bank Discussion Paper 196, World Bank, Washington.

Commander, Simon and *Christian Mumssen* (1998), Understanding Barter in Russia, European Bank for Reconstruction and Development, London, mimeo.

European Bank for Reconstruction and Development (1997), Transition Report, London, pp. 26-27.

Gaddy, Clifford G. and *Barry W. Ickes* (1998), Russia's Virtual Economy, in: Foreign Affairs, Vol. 77(5), pp. 53-67.

Hendley, Kathryn; Peter Murrell and *Randi Ryterman* (1999), Law Works in Russia: The Role of Legal Institutions in the Transactions of Russian Enterprise, mimeo, Wisconsin-Madison, Maryland and World Bank.

Huang, Haizhou; Dalia Marin and *Chenggang Xu* (2003), Financial Crisis, Economic Recovery and Banking Development in Russia and Other FSU Countries, International Monetary Fund Discussion Paper, International Monetary Fund, Washington.

Johnson, Simon; John McMillan and *Christopher Woodruff* (1999), Contract Enforcement in Transition, Cambridge, San Diego, mimeo.

Marin, Dalia (2000), Monetary Policy Does not Work in Russia's Barter Economy - German Banking as a Solution?, in: Economic Systems.

Marin, Dalia; Kaufmann Daniel and *Bogdan Gorochowskij* (2000), Barter in Transition Economies: Competing Explanations Confront Ukrainian Data, in: *Seabright, Paul* (ed.) The Vanishing Rouble, Cambridge, pp. 207-235.

Marin, Dalia and *Monika Schnitzer* (2002), Contracts in Trade and Transition: The Resurgence of Barter, Cambridge.

Marin, Dalia and *Monika Schnitzer* (2003), Disorganization and Financial Collapse, in: European Economic Review, forthcoming.

Organisation for Economic Cooperation and Development (1997), OECD Economic Surveys: Russian Federation 1997, Paris.

Organisation for Economic Cooperation and Development (2000), OECD Economic Surveys: Russian Federation 2000, Paris.

Russian Economic Barometer (1997), Survey of Industrial Firms, Institute for World Economy and International Relations, Moscow.

Rolf Hasse und Uwe Vollmer (eds.)
Incentives and Economic Behaviour
Schriften zu Ordnungsfragen der Wirtschaft · Band 76 · Stuttgart · 2005

Rational (Software-) Agents

Torsten Eymann

Contents

1. Towards the Information Systems of the 21st Century

The technological progress of computer technology gives rise to a change in fundamental design of information systems. Three development trends have the potential to change design, deployment and utilization of information systems on a broad basis.

The first one is *mobile computing*, which allows human users to access information services like newscasts, banking or communication from virtually every point on the globe. In the case of mobile computing, the access devices physically move with their owners and with them the access to IT services. A characterizing feature of mobile computing's *first phase* (*Müller, Eymann* and *Kreutzer* 2002) is that the notion or constitution of the service provisioning – apart from mobile access of the clients – does not differ from the stationary case. The related computer technologies are PDAs or mobile phones, which run modified versions of the same client software used for PCs.

Based on this achievement, the next technological step is *pervasive* or *ubiquitous computing*. These concepts reflect on having information technology invisibly embedded in the environment. The infiltrating device continuously interacts with the "smart" environment whilst in motion, using the uses environmental information for a permanent and seamless adaptation of its internal reality modelling to a constantly changing reality (*Mattern* 2001; *Banavar* and *Bernstein* 2002). The information devices greatly differ in their potential and resources, but can form and access "meta services" to compensate through communication with the environment. Ubiquitous computing thereby presents a *second phase*, in which devices offer each other services according to their means, i.e. are alternately available as server and client.

The miniaturization of technology is accompanied by an increasing networking of information devices, which can offer application services, storage or processor time to each other. *Grid computing* takes on the notion of the electricity grid and envisions large, complex computer networks that allow the ubiquitous usage of services requiring a otherwise huge amount of resources. In other words, like households can access all energy needs using the electricity network, computer grids connect large numbers of individual computers for information search, content download, parallel processing or data storage. Today's Grid computing is mainly used for distributed processing (e.g. for analysing particle accelerator experiments), while Peer-to-Peer-(P2P)-Computing similarly addresses distributed data storage and access (e.g. for multimedia files).

> "The common view of these technical developments is the global accessibility of the virtual information sphere, which leads to an 'omnipresence' of information, 'information overload', the loss of the differentiation between computerized and non-computerized items, and which ultimately creates information technology which 'weaves' into the fabric of everyday life until it is no longer distinguishable from it." (*Weiser* 1991).

For human users, these developments will cause a change in awareness, utilization and dealings with information technology. Computers which constantly signal for requiring user attention and interaction will create a need for "calm technology" (*Weiser* and *Brown* 1996), information technology that intercepts through a far-reaching autonomy of software.

Figure 1:   A layered model for decentralized information systems

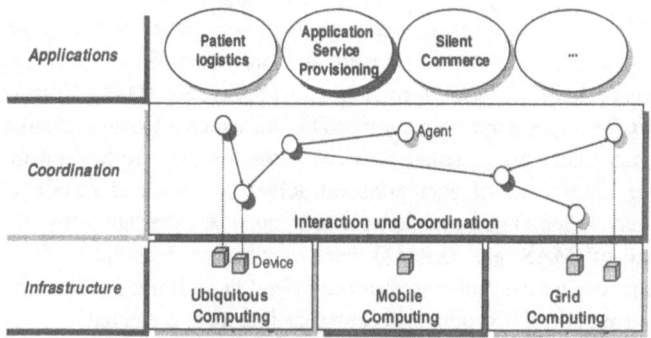

Figure 1 shows how these different technology infrastructures and the business applications (e.g. patient logistics (*Müller* et al. 2003), application service provisioning (*Ardaiz* et al. 2002) or silent commerce (*Schenker* 2000; *Cross* 2000)) can be divided in several technological layers. In the middle between technology and application sits a common software "coordination" layer which is responsible for interaction and coordination between those autonomous software objects. This coordination layer follows in its paradigms and mechanism the research done in software agents and multiagent systems (*Weiss* 1999).

The aim of this article is, to show how software agents can implement rational, strategic behaviour in order to achieve their design goals, which their human principals define. The large, complex and highly dynamical environments that ubiquitous computing or Grid computing makes technologically possible will neither provide complete information nor be accessible to analytical solutions. As a result, optimal results are hard to achieve, and require the adaptation of strategies. The question thus is how we can define strategies, which are rational both at the time of definition and during the (possibly infinite) lifetime of the software agent? If agents concurrently issue signals to effect the environment to change in a particular direction, will the resulting overall change be rational (explainable to human onlookers) at all?

2. Implementing Rational Strategies in Software Agents

Software agents are digital tools, which either support human users in decision-making or even act on their behalf. The IT user, who begins to drown in a sea of information everyday, soon comes up with the desire for an electronic authorised representative or agent, who automatically procures all information necessary to support a decision and subsequently acts in an optimal way without the user having to interact (*Eymann* 2003).

Visionaries have verbalized the notion of software agents since the early days of the Internet. In 1994, MIT's *Pattie Maes* painted a vision of intelligent and adaptive software agents who are capable of supporting humans in everyday tasks (*Maes* 1994). These expectations and application scenarios are now regarded as over-hyped; however, some productive concepts have survived and are scientifically investigated in the computer science field of *Distributed Artificial Intelligence* (DAI). Research in *Multi-Agent Systems* (MAS) is a specialization of DAI, in which a loosely coupled network of problem solvers that work together to solve problems that are beyond the individual capabilities or knowledge of each problem solver (*Durfee* and *Lesser* 1989). These problem solvers (agents) are autonomous and may be heterogeneous in nature. The characteristics of MAS are that (1) each agent has incomplete information, or capabilities for solving the problem, thus each agent has a limited viewpoint, (2) there is no global system control, (3) data is decentralised, and (4) computation is asynchronous (*Jennings, Sycara* and *Wooldridge* 1998).

In such systems, software agents work on their environment by (1) using sensors to acquire information, (2) build an internal world model out of the information aggregated over time, (3) make plans to change the sensed world model towards a favourable state, and (4) finally use effectors to push the environment to change in a desired direction (*Wooldridge* 1999).

Figure 2:   Software agents and the environment

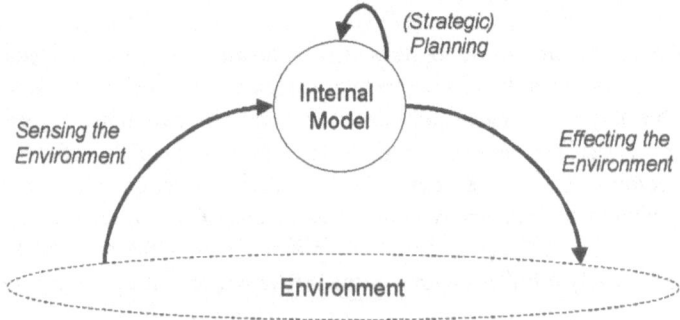

In an economic environment, software agents can assist human buyers and sellers in digital business processes to save transaction costs. Examples are price comparisons between different suppliers in the on- and offline world (*Youll* et al. 2000); the networked laser printer which automatically buys toner when needed (*Cross* 2000); the mobile fare payment when entering the train using PDA or mobile phone, the payment of web services by networked clients in the Grid (*Ardaiz* et al. 2002); or built-to-order adaptive supply chain control concepts using software agents (*Living Systems AG* 2001). Such specialized agents may be described as *Digital Business Agents* (DBAs) (*Eymann* 2003).

If the environment depicted in Figure 2 is an economic information sphere, it holds information about the scarcity or abundance of goods and services. By receiving price signals, the DBA builds an internal model of the current situation regarding supply and demand, and compares this to a design goal. This goal is defined either by the human principal or the erstwhile software designer, and will be derived from the self-interest of the human principal, for three logical reasons (*Rasmusson* and *Janson* 1999). If (1) human users can define their own agents, they will implement them to follow their own self-interest; (2) if human users can choose between self-interested agents or ones, which enhance other's utility at their expense, they will choose the first; (3) if human users can only use software agents which increase other's utility, they will use them only if this is better than not using them at all.

In an economic environment, this goal will thus be utility maximization. In its simplest form, the DBA will compare different suppliers for the same good or services based on prices, and choose the cheapest. Further using Figure 2, the DBA acts by issuing a bid to the cheapest supplier, while the more expensive competitors receive either a rejection or no information at all. This action tends to have an effect on the environment, as the cheapest supplier gets a reward and the others get none.

In more complicated scenarios, agents can issue a stream of offer and counter-offer messages, following an automated negotiation protocol, e.g. *Rubinstein's* alternating offers model (*Rubinstein* 1982; *Rosenschein* and *Zlotkin* 1994). The offer sent to the opponent is an effector, which has the intention to draw the opponent towards a more favourable negotiation compromise.

If this negotiation is one-dimensionally based on prices alone, the strategies of the internal model calculate offer prices to propose to a trade negotiations opponent, in order to achieve a maximum utility gain. Note that one assumption was large, complex environments with incomplete information, so using auctioneers (*Wellman* 1996) or arbitrators (*Tesch* and *Fankhauser* 1999) both reaches technical limits of scalability, and does not rule out strategic behaviour anyway (*Sandholm* 1996).

The strategy model itself can be based on rule-based, argumentative, game-theoretic or heuristic-adaptive approaches (*Jennings* et al. 2001; *Kraus* 1997). The choice of strategy type depends largely on the characteristics of the problem domain. An agent-based silent commerce scenario with direct interaction constitutes a non-accessible, partly deterministic, discrete, highly dynamic and non-episodic environment (*Russel* and *Norvig* 1995):

–   *Not accessible:* Accessibility denotes the ability of the agent to assess the complete state of the environment by using sensory input. In the scenarios considered here, the agent frequently receives both unsolicited information and concrete responses to offers. However, it is not possible to get insights into the internal decision processes of other agents. In total, the agent's world model is made up of historic, sporadic and infrequent information.

– *Partly deterministic:* The use of a common negotiation protocol leads to deterministic states of the negotiation under predictable conditions. However, the behaviour of the negotiation opponents in response to a particular offer is not predictable and can comprise a large, potentially infinite number of possible actions.

– *Discrete:* The possible actions of a negotiating agent are limited to choosing a price from the set of the natural numbers or terminating the negotiation by either acceptance or rejection.

– *Dynamic:* The internal model and thus the strategy of the negotiators may change both during and between negotiations using adaptive mechanisms. It is not predictable whether the response of an opponent will be equal to earlier responses when facing the same negotiation situation.

– *Non-Episodic:* Successive negotiations are linked by budget restraints and feedback propagation of success or failure of the current action decision set, even if the negotiations can be considered independent otherwise. In particular, the outcome of a single negotiation depends only on the choice of strategy parameter set at the beginning of the negotiation process.

In such a complex, unpredictable environment with possibly thousands of acting and negotiating agents, rule-based or game-theoretic strategies alone are considered to be not realistically applicable (*Kraus* 1997). It is possible to equip heuristics with some economic background e.g. on reputation and cheating of opponents (*Padovan* et al. 2001), or common market and negotiation behaviour (*Sackmann* 2003). However, these heuristics are geared toward a present situation of the environment. Their ability to maximize utility will decrease as the environment changes over time. This leads to the necessity to enhance heuristics with adaptation capabilities:

> "In future applications in e-commerce, multi agent systems will need to be much more open-ended and dynamic [...]. In particular it is important for the negotiating agents to be able to adapt their strategies to deal with changing opponents, changing topics and concerns, and changing user profiles." (*Gerding, Bragt* and *La Poutré* 2000).

3. Supply Chain Management using Software Agents

This section presents experiments done in the multi-agent system AVALANCHE and its successor B2B-OS (*Eymann* 2003). The application example is a simple model supply chain management problem. Software agents here represent enterprises of the wood-processing industry at various net product stages (lumberjack, carpenter and cabinetmaker, see Figure 2) and independently carry out business activities on behalf of their user.

They operate as automated producers (*Kephart, Hanson* and *Greenwald* 2000), who purchase the necessary input factors from other agents on the electronic marketplaces, transform them through a (simulated) production process into an intermediate or end product and, in turn, sell the manufactured product to other agents. The agents map and alter the current state of their environment through the direct communication of price information via purchasing and sales offers with other agents or through interfaces to databases, catalogs, auctioneers or other service providers. Their internal model maps the actual state of the market and decides here on the type of action based on a heuristic strategy. This strategy is adapting using machine learning mechanisms (*Goldberg* 1993), and this constant revision of strategies leads to a co-evolution of software agent strategies, a stabilization of prices throughout the system and self-regulating coordination patterns (*Eymann* 2001). The resulting patterns are comparable to those observed in human market negotiation experiments (*Pruitt* 1981).

Figure 3:   AVALANCHE **supply chain model**

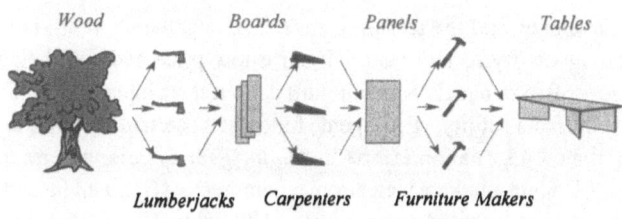

Wood   *Boards*   *Panels*   *Tables*

Lumberjacks   *Carpenters*   *Furniture Makers*

During the information phase (*Müller, Eymann* and *Kreutzer* 2002; *Lindemann* and *Schmid* 1999), the purchasers and/or sellers choose potential transaction partners through random selection. In the negotiation phase, an agent initiates a bilateral price negotiation and alternating bids are exchanged according to a monotonic concession protocol (*Rosenschein* and *Zlotkin* 1994) until an agreement is reached or negotiations are broken off (see Figure 3). The buyer agent initiates a negotiation by proposing a seller, whose address was obtained from reading the white board, sending a *propose* message containing the sender A's identity, the receiver B's identity and the particular offer price x. The receiver B has now the choice between downright accepting the price, making a counter-offer, or refusing to further negotiate at all. Whether the state transaction from state a to either states b (propose), c (accept), or i (refuse) is executed, depends on the action decision made in the agent's internal model. The negotiation continues until either a deal has been landed (state g) or one of the agents has unilaterally decided to refuse further negotiation (state i).

Figure 4:   **Negotiation protocol between two agents A and B**

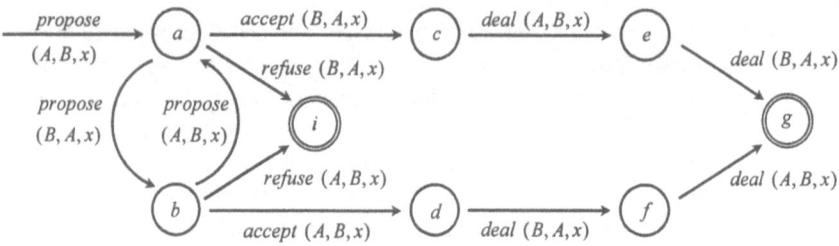

In the control and adaptation phase, the agents carry out and monitor the execution of the transaction. The transaction price realized alters the subjective estimation of the market price for both agents with corresponding feedback on the strategy. The initial price with which an agent enters into the negotiation is increased or decreased for the purpose of utility maximization.

3.1. A Heuristic Negotiation Strategy for Software Agents

The goal of the agents, and the reason to engage in negotiation at all, is to maximize their budget. The agents try to buy materials for a low price and sell their products at high price to other software agents which in turn use these as input goods. To maximize the spread and thus its utility, the agent follows a certain negotiation strategy. Comparable automated negotiation efforts in *Multi-Agent Systems* can be found in the research context of agent-mediated electronic commerce (*Guttman* and *Maes* 1998; *Sierra* 2000) and market-oriented programming (*Wellman* 1996). Human negotiation uses parameters such as demand level, concession, and concession rate:

> "A bargainer's demand level can be thought of as the level of benefit to the self associated with the current offer or demand. A concession is a change of offer in the supposed direction of the other party's interests that reduces the level of benefit sought. Concession rate is the speed at which demand level declines over time. [...] These definitions [... are] unproblematic, when only one issue or underlying value is being considered, as in a simple wage or price negotiation." (*Pruitt* 1981).

The human principal chooses the initial values of these parameters as part of the strategy definition during the initialization of the software agent. In the real world, the values are influenced by determinants such as expectations about the other's ultimate demand, position and image loss, limit and level of aspiration and time pressure (*Pruitt* 1981). Whatever strategy will be used, these parameters will have to be encoded in some way to make it useful.

The AVALANCHE agents implement a heuristic-adaptive strategy based on a stochastic automaton, in which action paths are taken depending on stochastic probes against certain internal parameters. As their human owners will define the strategy of DBAs, the stochastic automaton approach attempts to capture the relevant parameters and sets them in relation to each other. Earlier work in agent-mediated electronic commerce used rule-based (*Kreifelt* and *Von Martial* 1991) or price-curve models (*Chavez* and *Maes* 1996). From an economic aspect, probabilistic models have been experimentally found to outperform simple deterministic models (*Erev* and *Roth* 1998); even strategy models with "zero intelligence" (*Cliff* and *Bruten* 1998) have been found to perform quite well in Multi-Agent Systems. From a technical aspect, the strategy calculation is fast, simple, and easy to define. In AVALANCHE, a combination of six distinct parameters, collectively called the *genotype*, describes the strategy:

$$(1) \qquad G = \begin{pmatrix} p\_acq \\ del\_change \\ del\_jump \\ p\_sat \\ w\_mem \\ p\_rep \end{pmatrix}$$

Acquisitiveness (*p_acq*) defines the probability of maintaining the agent's own last offer. The lower the acquisitiveness value, the higher the average concession rate. Whether an agent concedes in an actual situation is subject to a stochastic probe against this parameter. If *RND* is a random variable and p_s^t the new offer price of seller S at time t, the following computation is done:

$$(2) \qquad p_s = \begin{cases} RND < p\_acq : p_s^t = p_s^{t-1} \\ RND \geq p\_acq : p_s^t = p_s^{t-1} - \Delta p \end{cases}.$$

If the agent concedes, the *del_change* parameter calculates the amount of the price concession Δp between two negotiation steps. Seller S and buyer B calculate a percentage from the price difference of their original offers:

$$(3) \qquad \Delta p = (p_S - p_B) \times del\_change .$$

To reflect increased knowledge about the market price of one good and simultaneously to maximize income, the agents will set their initial demand level P for the start of the negotiation to the last agreement price $p_{B=S}$, modified by the relative value of *del_jump*:

(4) $$P = p_{B=S} \times del\_jump.$$

The *satisfaction parameter* *(p_sat)* determines if an agent will drop out from an ongoing negotiation. The more steps the negotiation takes, or the more excessive the partner's offers are, the sooner the negotiation will be discontinued. Effectively, this parameter creates time pressure by continuously comparing the market price stored in the memory parameter with the actual offer (shown here for the buyer):

(5)
$$\begin{cases} negotiate: p_S > mem \wedge RND > p\_sat \\ reject: p_S > 2mem \\ accept: p_S < mem \end{cases}.$$

All price information received from negotiations computes into a subjective market price for each agent, which modifies the parameter *memory* using a weighted exponential average with weight *w_mem*:

(6) $$mem_t = p \times w_{mem} + mem_{t-1} \times (1 - w_{mem}).$$

Reputation finally *(p_rep)* affects the cooperative behaviour of the software agents. In this article, all agents are assumed to cooperate; for other cases, see *Padovan* et al. (2001).

The heterogeneity is achieved, if needed, by a uniform random distribution of the initial strategy parameter values, which effectively assigns a different strategy to each agent. The "fitness" denominator for the individual agent's strategy is obviously currency: An agent, which is faster and/or fitter in trading than another will have a relatively higher income. Apart from costs incurred for materials and production, the agents have to pay utilization fees, e.g. for resources like computer memory, communication bandwidth and processor time. An agent who does nothing will run out of money after a short time (go bankrupt) and be discarded from the system.

3.2. Experimental Results

To test the behaviour of the AVALANCHE system we conduct several test series. Every series consists of several experiment runs, which under similar conditions lead to comparable outcome patterns. In the current implementation we run a generator program, an experimental control object, a single marketplace and 50 trading agents of each type (for a total of 250 agents) in parallel on a Pentium PC under Windows NT for about 10 minutes. The following presentations all show similar patterns when repeatedly starting with the same initial values. However, absolute price levels or points in time have no meaning since they change in every run.

We start with some simple parameter combinations and subsequently move on to experiments that are more complex. The first experiment shown here has homogenous strategies, which means that all agents are equipped with an identical Genotype and there is no variation of parameter values in the population: *p_acq* = *0.50*, *del_change* = *0.25*, *del_jump* = *0.15*, *p_sat* = *0.75*, *w_mem* = *0.2*, and *p_rep* = *1*. The agents hold no stock, but some initial equity money. Every 10 milliseconds a new "wood" is produced by any producer agent. The consumer agents never run out of money. Initial goods valuations are defined equally for every agent type (e.g. 25 money units for boards).

Using the simple picture of Figure 5, showing the dynamics of the coordination mechanism, we explain the presentation charts. The horizontal axis measures the time in milliseconds, the vertical axis shows the price level. Every dot in the chart points out time and agreement price of a transaction, e.g. the *x*-value of a gray triangle marks the time when some carpenter software agent has sold a table to a cabinetmaker software agent for *y*-value price. Different gray scales and symbols represent the type of goods as indicated by the legend, which shows the supply chain from top to bottom. In the chart, this succession has been turned upside down since woods are sold for the lowest price and tables for the highest. To make the graphic comparable there is a price ceiling for tables at 120 money units, which can be seen in later experiments. The time lag at the beginning is caused by software initialization and initial negotiation until the first goods are moved up the supply chain.

In Figure 5 it is not possible for a single agent to gain an advantage, since all agents possess an identical static negotiation strategy. The price levels do not substantially change during the course of the experiment.

In the next experiment, the carpenter agents are initialized with a "greedier" negotiation strategy than all other types. The equipment of only one agent type (carpenters) with *p_acq* = *0.6*, and all others with *p_acq* = *0.4*, leads to a picture of winners and losers (see Figure 5, the vertical white stripes in the figure are experimental artifacts caused by the Windows NT environment and have no effect on the outcome). If the concession rate is lowered (by raising *p_acq*), this leads to a dramatic decrease of the number of transactions: If the probability of dropping out of a negotiation is greater than the probability of conceding, lesser compromises are reached during the same time span.

Figure 5:   Price dynamics using homogeneous strategies

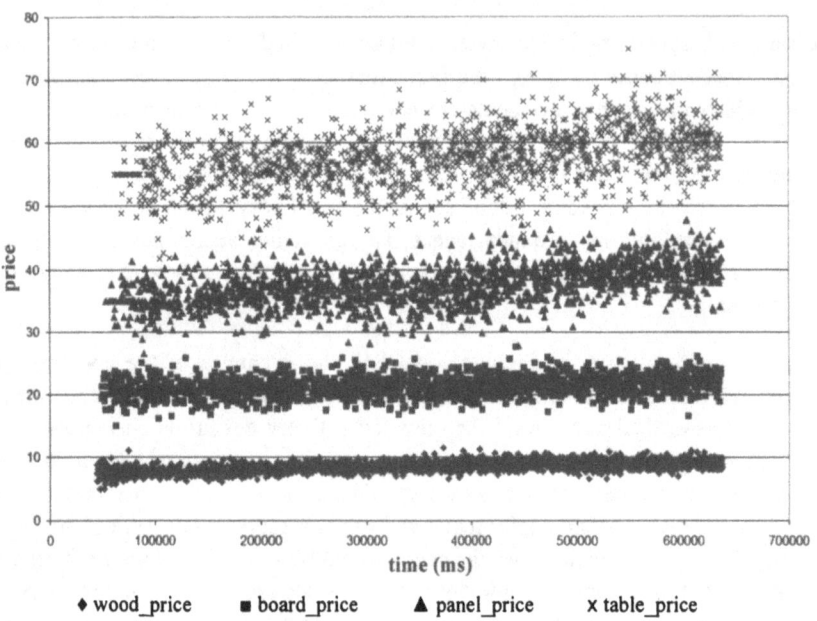

Since the other agent types concede faster than the carpenters, the latter are able to increase their income (the spread between board prices and panel prices) at the expense of both lumberjacks and cabinetmakers. It appears to be a dominating strategy to set the agent's acquisitiveness as high as possible as, at least higher as any other agent it might trade with, and in fact this is where the gains of the carpenters come from. In an environment without evolutionary learning and open markets, the higher acquisitiveness of the carpenters is a dominating strategy. However, most of these experiments abort early, because the lumberjacks and cabinetmakers run out of money and are thus not able to continue the supply chain – in this case, the victory was short-lived.

3.3. Adapting to Changing Market Situations

By varying the setting of the Genotype parameters in subsequent experimental runs, we can show how dominant parameter combinations either succeed or are counterbalanced. The negotiation profit gained from a specific *genotype* is correlated to the relative setting of other agent's strategies, not the absolute values. "Learning" the right values relative to the other agents is thus essential to gain a higher profit in the future. In Figure 6, the inability of the agents to change their strategy affects both winners and losers – the other agents should raise their own acquisitiveness setting to gain more profit, while the carpenters could lower their setting to conduct more transactions within the same time to increase turnover.

The design goal of AVALANCHE's learning algorithm was to avoid a centralized fitness evaluator with perfect knowledge about each agent's performance, in analogy to the decentralized coordination concept. The chosen implementation uses a decentralized evolutionary algorithm taken from *Smith* and *Taylor* (1998), which is based on posted information about the success of transactions. The *genotype* has been described above, the phenotype is the witnessed strategy and the fitness is the profit over time.

Figure 6: **Different concession rates lead to different profits**

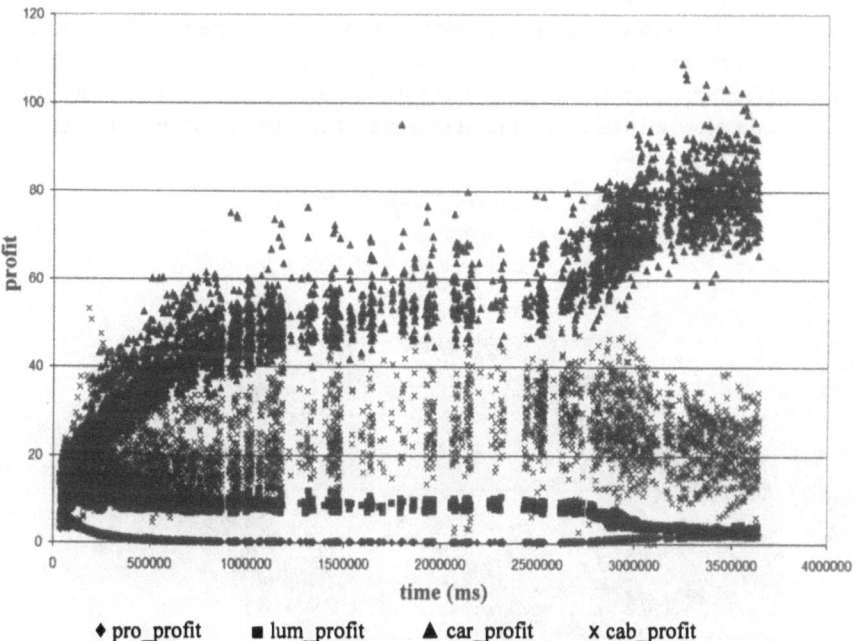

In AVALANCHE, every agent sends one *plumage* object after a successful transaction, advertising its average income and its genes to one random agent of the same type. This can be interpreted as someone receiving insider information about otherwise private deal information of someone else. As the information is not publicly available, each agent will collect over time a different list of received *plumages*. Now begin the four phases, common in evolutionary algorithms (*Goldberg* 1993). Upon having received a fixed number of 15 *plumages*, every agent ranks them and selects the *plumage* with the highest average income attached (evaluation and selection phase). The *genotype* of the sender is extracted from the *plumage* and compared with the agent's own *genotype* (reproduction phase). This *plumage* will then be crossed over with the agent's own strategy genes, slightly mutated, and "planted" into a new agent which then enters the marketplace (recombination and mutation phase).

In effect, the evolutionary algorithm relegates unsuccessful agents/strategies and promotes successful agents/strategies, changing the composition of the population over time. A variant of this mechanism (not shown here) could replace the *genotype* of the agent with a modified version, which creates a constant sized population of immortal, but learning agents.

Figure 6 has shown how heterogeneous strategies of the agents affected the overall behaviour of the system, in case there is no evolution. In contrast, Figure 7 shows the results of an experiment where economic effects are combined with evolutionary learning. The carpenters were, as before, equipped with a lesser probability to make price concessions, and this is again evident in the first half of the experiment run: The spread between the second (boards) and third (panels) price curve increases. But this time, the lumberjack and cabinetmaker agents are (after some time) not only able to withstand the pressure, but to turn the tables and to dominate the carpenter agents.

Figure 7:   Price level development with evolution

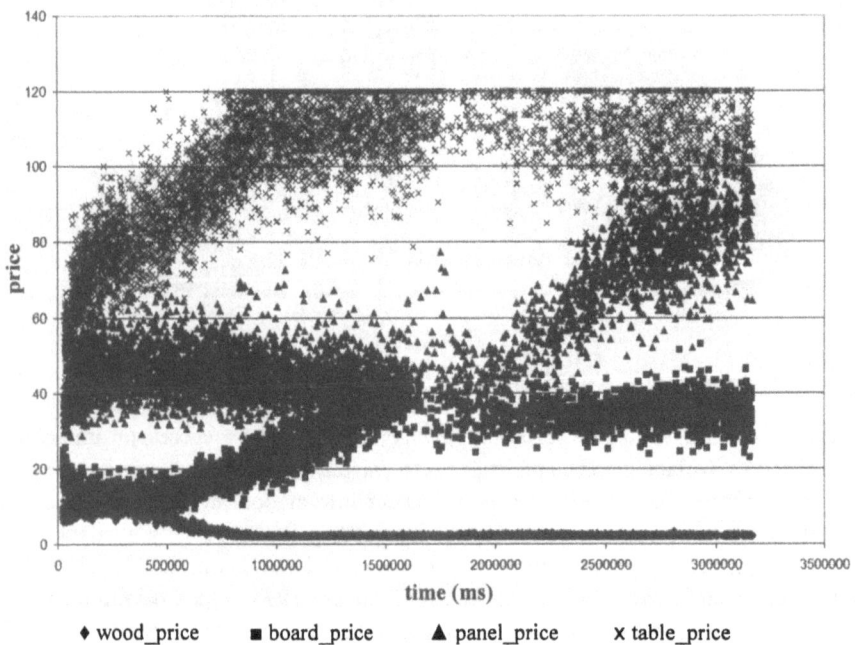

This is graphically displayed in Figure 8, where every curve represents the average acquisitiveness values of a specific agent type over time. The topmost curve at the beginning represents the carpenters, and one can see that their initially high average of the acquisitiveness parameter soon declines too much.

After the first half of the experiment, the carpenters end up with the lowest setting of all three inner agent types. At the same time, the lumberjack and cabinetmaker agents are able to co-evolve and raise their acquisitiveness setting. At around 1500 seconds in the earlier Figure 7, the spread between board and panel prices had finally vanished and with it the profits of the carpenter agents. In Figure 8 at that time, the average acquisitiveness setting of the carpenter agents reaches the lowest value compared to the other agent types.

This picture changes again in the second half of both charts, when the cabinetmaker agents learn and raise their acquisitiveness again. Similar to the beginning, now the cabinetmaker, and to a lesser extent, the lumberjack agents reduce their acquisitiveness values as shown in Figure 8. The result can be immediately seen in Figure 7: The carpenter agents gain ground, the lumberjack agents are able to withstand the pressure and keep their profit situation, and the cabinetmaker agents lose everything gained in the first half of the experiment run. In summary, a highly dynamic pattern of co-evolution arises, where learning successful parameter settings allows other participants to survive and prosper early while dominating strategies are counterbalanced. Because the size and strategies of the population constantly change, this result will probably never reach a static endpoint, like an evolutionary function optimizer does.

Figure 8:   Evolutionary development of the acquisitiveness parameter

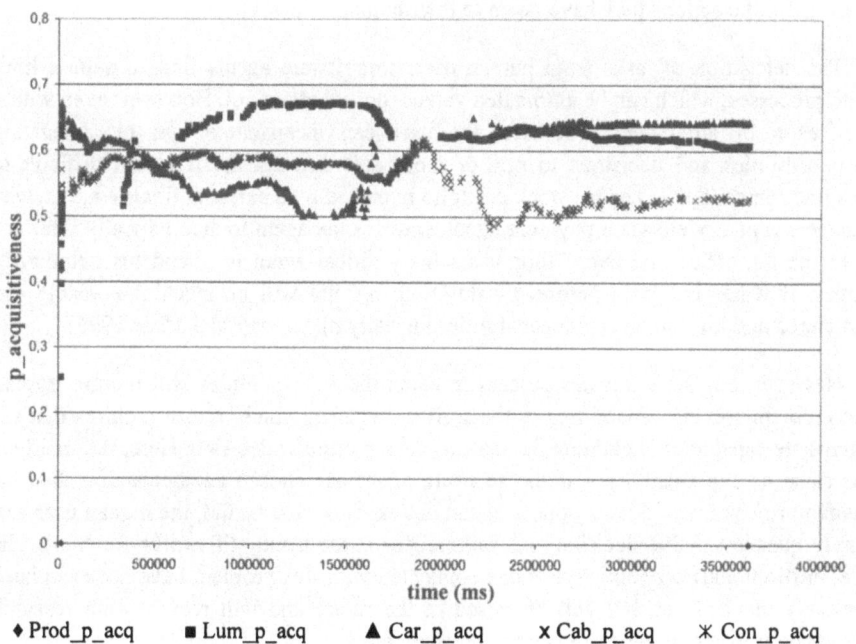

4.   The Future of (Rational) Software Agents

The AVALANCHE implementation presented here is an experimental prototype of an electronic market environment with automated negotiating software agents. It is not a valid and productive business application, but can be used to show how such market environments may look like in the future. On one hand, by abstracting from the concrete technology and the business application (see Figure 1), the prototype can be used for experimental research and simulation of different coordination problems in economics. The combination of economic models of individual behaviour with an information technology which allows implementing individual behaviour, creates the fruitful research field of *Agent-based Computational Economics* (ACE) (*Tesfatsion* 1997; *Kearney* and *Merlat* 1999; *Vulkan* and *Jennings* 1999; *Wellman* 1996). Once the starting conditions and interaction paths are set, all subsequent events are initiated and driven by agent-agent- and agent-environment interaction (*Lane* 1993), without the researcher influencing the development, e.g. by externally computing and feeding back an equilibrium price.

On the other hand, those *Multi-Agent systems* are a first step to future information systems and business applications. The release of such systems "in the wild" is still controversial and surely needs many laboratory experiments (*Kephart, Hanson* and *Sairamesh* 1998). Two key questions are, to what extent human users can or should delegate tasks to software agents, and if software agents will be able to explain the reasons for the actions they have taken to their human principal.

The delegation of tasks from human users to software agents finds a natural limit with processes, which can be automated versus those that are not. However, even within the realm of automated processes, the user can incapacitate him by delegating responsibilities and decisions to one or more software agents. It is not difficult to imagine someone who has his stock portfolio managed by a personal finance agent, who transfers capital yield via a payment agent, uses his tax agent to automatically interface with the tax office and every four years his political agent to attend his democratic duties. If it has not been before, by this time his life will be machine-readable and structured and his own decision capabilities virtually nil (*Lanier* and *Maes* 1996).

However, any slow transfer process to reach those possibilities will require trust in the problem-solving capabilities of the software agents, which in turn requires that the agents are capable of explaining the reasons for a particular decision. Here, rationality is the same as explainability – if the software agent has chosen another action than his human principal would have done *and* can not explain what he did, the human user will surely question if that decision was rational (or if the agent still works for him). The (neo-institutional) economic questions connected with this problem have not even been remotely touched yet, but will be raised in the future and will require joint research efforts between economists and computer scientists.

References

Ardaiz, Oscar; Felix Freitag; Leandro Navarro; Torsten Eymann and *Michael Reinicke* (2002), CatNet - Catallactic Mechanisms for Service Control and Resource Allocation in Large Scale Application-Layer Networks, Proc. Workshop on Global and Peer-to-Peer Computing on Large Scale Distributed Systems, 2nd IEEE/ACM International Symposium on Cluster Computing and the Grid, Berlin, May 2002.

Banavar, Guruduth and *Abraham Bernstein* (2002), Software Infrastructure and Design Challenges for Ubiquitous Computing, in: Communications of the ACM, Vol. 45, No. 12, pp. 92-96.

Chavez, Anthony and *Pattie Maes* (1996), Kasbah: An Agent Marketplace for Buying and Selling Goods, Proceedings of the First International Conference on Practical Applications of Agents and Multiagent Systems, London, pp. 75-90.

Cliff, David and *J. Bruten* (1998), Less than Human: Simple Adaptive Trading Agents for CDA Markets, Proceedings of the IFAC Symposium on Computation in Economics, Finance, and Engineering: Economic Systems (CEFES'98), June 1998-July 1998, no page numbering.

Cross, Kim (2000), Intershop around the corner, in: Business 2.0, May 2000.

Durfee, Edmund H. and *V. R. Lesser* (1989), Negotiating Task Decomposition and Allocation Using Partial Global Planning, in: *Les Gasser* and *M. Huhns* (eds.), Distributed Artificial Intelligence, San Mateo, CA., pp. 229-244.

Erev, Ido and *Alvin E. Roth* (1998), Predicting How People Play Games - Reinforcement Learning in Experimental Games with Unique, Mixed Strategy Equilibria, in: American Economic Review, Vol. 88, No. 4, pp. 848-881.

Eymann, Torsten (2001), Co-Evolution of Bargaining Strategies in a Decentralized Multi-Agent System, AAAI Fall 2001 Symposium on Negotiation Methods for Autonomous Cooperative Systems, Falmouth, MA, pp. 126-134.

Eymann, Torsten (2003), Digitale Geschäftsagenten, Springer Xpert.press, Heidelberg.

Gerding, Enrico H.; David D. B. Bragt and *J. A. La Poutré* (2000), Scientific Approaches and Techniques for Negotiation - a Game Theoretic and Artificial Intelligence Perspective, Centrum voor Wiskunde en Informatica, Report, No. SEN-R0005.

Goldberg, D. (1993), Genetic Algorithms in Search, Optimization and Machine Learning, Reading MA.

Guttman, Robert H. and *Pattie Maes* (1998), Agent-mediated Integrative Negotiation for Retail Electronic Commerce, in: Proceedings of the Workshop on Agent Mediated Electronic Trading, Minneapolis.

Jennings, Nicholas R.; Katia Sycara and *Michael J. Wooldridge* (1998), A Roadmap of Agent Research and Development, in: Journal of Autonomous Agents and Multi-Agent Systems, Vol. 1, No. 1, pp. 275-306.

Jennings, Nicholas R.; Peyman Faratin; Alessio R. Lomuscio; Carles Sierra and *Michael J. Wooldridge* (2001), Automated Negotiation: Prospects, Methods and Challenges, in: International Journal of Group Decision and Negotiation, Vol. 10, No. 2, pp. 1-20.

Kearney, Paul J. and *Walter Merlat* (1999), Modelling Market-based Decentralised Management Systems, in: BT Technology Journal, Vol. 17, No. 4, pp. 145-156.

Kephart, Jeffrey O.; James E. Hanson and *Amy R. Greenwald* (2000), Dynamic Pricing by Software Agents, in: Computer Networks, Vol. 32, No. 6, pp. 731-752.

Kephart, Jeffrey O.; James E. Hanson and *Jakka Sairamesh* (1998), Price and Niche Wars in a Free-Market Economy of Software Agents, in: Artificial Life Journal, Vol. 4, No. 1, pp. 1-23.

Kraus, Sarit (1997), Negotiation and Cooperation in Multi-agent Environments, in: Artificial Intelligence, Vol. 94, pp. 79-97.

Kreifelt, T. and *F. Von Martial* (1991), A Negotiation Framework for Autonomous Agents, in: *Yves Demazeau* and *Jörg P. Müller* (eds.), Proceedings of Decentralized Artificial Intelligence II, Amsterdam.

Lane, David A. (1993), Artificial worlds and economics (Part I), in: Journal of Evolutionary Economics, Vol. 3, pp. 89-107.

Lanier, Jaron and *Pattie Maes* (1996), Intelligent Agents = Stupid Humans?, in: HotWired, Vol. 29, July, pp. 15-24.

Lindemann, Markus A. and *Beat Schmid* (1999), A Framework for Specifying, Building, and Operating Electronic Markets, in: International Journal of Electronic Commerce, Vol. 3, No. 2, pp. 7-22.

Living Systems AG (2001), Living Markets Technische Dokumentation, Living Systems AG, Report No. 1.03, Donaueschingen.

Maes, Pattie (1994), Agents that Reduce Work and Information Overload, in: Communications of the ACM, Vol. 37, No. 7, pp. 30-40.

Mattern, Friedemann (2001), Ubiquitous Computing - Der Trend zur Informatisierung und Vernetzung aller Dinge, in: *Gerhard Rossbach* (ed.), Mobile Internet. Tagungsband 6. Deutscher Internet-Kongress, Heidelberg, pp. 107-119.

Müller, Günter; Torsten Eymann and *Michael Kreutzer* (2002), Telematik- und Kommunikationssysteme in der vernetzten Wirtschaft, Oldenbourg, München.

Müller, Günter; Michael Kreutzer; Moritz Strasser; Torsten Eymann; Adolf Hohl; Norbert Nopper; Stefan Sackmann and *Vlad Coroama* (2003), Geduldige Technologie für ungeduldige Patienten: Führt Ubiquitous Computing zu mehr Selbstbestimmung?, in: *Friedemann Mattern* (ed.), Total Vernetzt. Living in a Smart Environment, Heidelberg, pp. 83-97.

Padovan, Boris; Stefan Sackmann; Torsten Eymann and *Ingo Pippow* (2001), A Prototype for an Agent-based Secure Electronic Marketplace including Reputation Tracking Mechanisms, in: *Ralph H. Sprague* (ed.), Proceedings of the 34th Hawaiian International Conference on Systems Sciences, Outrigger Wailea Resort, Maui, Jan. 2001, pp. 407-415.

Pruitt, Dean G. (1981), Negotiation Behavior, New York.

Rasmusson, Lars and *Sverker Janson* (1999), Agents, Self-interest and Electronic Markets, in: Knowledge Engineering Review, Vol. 14, No. 2, pp. 143-150.

Rosenschein, Jeffrey S. and *Gilad Zlotkin* (1994), Rules of Encounter - Designing Conventions for Automated Negotiation Among Computers, Cambridge.

Rubinstein, Ariel (1982), Perfect Equilibrium in a Bargaining Model, in: Econometrica, Vol. 50, pp. 97-109.

Russel, S. J. and *P. Norvig* (1995), Artificial Intelligence. A Modern Approach, Englewood Cliffs.

Sackmann, Stefan (2003), Bilaterale Preisverhandlungen von Software-Agenten - Ein Modell und System zur Analyse des marktplatzspezifischen Verhandlungsspielraums, Wiesbaden.

Sandholm, Tuomas W. (1996), Limitations of the Vickrey Auction in Computational Multiagent Systems, Proceedings of the Second International Conference on Multiagent Systems (ICMAS-96), Keihanna Plaza, Kyoto, Japan, pp. 299-306.

Schenker, Jennifer L. (2000), The Trillion-Dollar Secret, in: TIME Magazine, Vol. 155, No. 8.

Sierra, Carles (2000), Agent-mediated Electronic Commerce: Scientific and Technological Roadmap, Institute for Information and Computing Siences, Utrecht University, Working Paper.

Smith, Robert E. and *Nick Taylor* (1998), A Framework for Evolutionary Computation in Agent-Based Systems, in: *C. Looney* and *J. Castaing* (eds.), Proceedings of the 1998 International Conference on Intelligent Systems.

Tesch, Thomas and *Peter Fankhauser* (1999), Arbitration and Matchmaking for Agents with Conflicting Interests, in: *Matthias Klush; Onn Shehory* and *Gerhard Weiß* (eds.), Cooperative Information Agents III, Heidelberg, pp. 323-334.

Tesfatsion, Leigh (1997), How Economists can get Alife, in: *W. B. Arthur; S. Durlauf* and *David A. Lane* (eds.), The Economy as a Evolving Complex System II, Redwood City, CA, pp. 533-564.

Vulkan, Nir and *Nickolas R. Jennings* (1999), Efficient Mechanisms for the Supply of Services in Multi-Agent Environments, Proceedings of 1st International Conference on Information and Computation Economies, Charlestown, South Carolina, pp. 1-10.

Weiser, Mark (1991), The Computer for the Twenty-First Century, in: Scientific American, Vol. 265, No. 3, pp. 94-104.

Weiser, Mark and *J. S. Brown* (1996), The Coming Age of Calm Technology, Unpublished Work.

Weiss, Gerhard (1999), Multiagent Systems, Cambridge, MA.

Wellman, Michael P. (1996), Market-Oriented Programming: Some Early Lessons, in: *Scott H. Clearwater* (ed.), Market-Based Control: A Paradigm for Distributed Resource Allocation, Singapore, pp. 74-95.

Wooldridge, Michael J. (1999), Intelligent Agents, in: *Gerhard Weiss* (ed.), Multiagent Systems, Cambridge, MA, pp. 27-78.

Youll, Jim; Joan Morris; Raffi Krikorian and *Pattie Maes* (2000), Impulse: Location-based Agent Assistance, Proceedings of the Fourth International Conference on Autonomous Agents (Agents 2000), Barcelona, June 2000.

Rolf Hasse und Uwe Vollmer (eds.)
Incentives and Economic Behaviour
Schriften zu Ordnungsfragen der Wirtschaft · Band 76 · Stuttgart · 2005

Monetary Policy and Bank Lending in Japan:
An Agency-based Approach

Diemo Dietrich

Contents

1. Introduction

In the 1990s, the Japanese banking industry experienced the sharpest crisis since World War II. Most economists agree that this crisis was a result of a combination of the slow and incomplete deregulation of the Japanese financial system in the 1980s and of the monetary tightening in the late 1980s.[1] The diffident deregulation of financial markets resulted in an asset price inflation, which was accompanied – or even driven – by a sharp increase of bank lending to the real estate industry.[2] For example, the proportion of bank loans to the real estate industry increased from 6 % in 1982 to 12 % in 1990 (*Hoshi* 2001). However, as a consequence of the tight monetary policy, the asset price bubble burst in the early 1990s, with which the amount of nonperforming or bad loans increased vigorously from Yen 12.6 trillion in March 1993 to Yen 30.0 trillion in September 1998; since that time it remained at 7 % of GDP (*Hoshi* and *Kashyap* 2000). These developments have affected the capital position of Japanese banks adversely.[3]

In 1996, both short-term and long-term nominal interest rates began to fall, which can broadly be interpreted as an attempt of monetary policy to reactivate the real economy. At least two different arguments have been discussed in the literature to explain why such a policy has failed to succeed: Firstly, the standard Keynesian position argues that the Japanese economy has been captured in a liquidity trap (*Krugman* 1998; *McKinnon* 2000). Secondly, the prudential regulation literature suggests that unsound Japanese banks have been unable to transmit monetary impulses properly. This view is referred to as the capital crunch hypothesis (*Bernanke* and *Lown* 1991) which argues that, if regulatory capital requirements for banks were binding, they would not allow for increasing bank lending even in case of a loose monetary policy (*Bolton* and *Freixas* 2001). Prima facie, this argument seems to meet the facts: Since 1997 the growth of the Japanese money stock (M2+CD) has been mainly (and to an increasing degree) driven by banks' safe claims on treasury accounts and not by risky lending to private nonfinancial enterprises and individuals (*Okina* 1999). However, bank lending has been actually decreasing by nearly 2 % on average and this makes the capital crunch argument perhaps less powerful.

We do not think that the Keynesian story actually resolves the Japanese puzzle at all since this requires taking any financial and real asset as perfect substitutes (*Meltzer* 2000). Therefore, Keynesian IS/LM-style models seem not to be a proper framework to study the special role of bank loans in monetary policy transmission in general and to

---

[1] *Kanaya* and *Woo* (2000) provide a survey of the sources of the Japanese banking crisis.

[2] There are doubts that the price movements in the Japanese real estate industry reflect a bubble. Nevertheless, from 1980 to 1990 prices for real estate rose almost 350 percent despite the low CPI-inflation (*Herring* and *Wachter* 1999).

[3] The loss of major banks' total capital base between 1990 and 1996 was about Yen 20 trillion or nearly 30 % respectively (*Woo* 1999).

explain structural effects of monetary policy on banks' asset portfolios in particular. But even the capital crunch hypothesis reflects only half of the story once we allow for bank capital requirements to be market based and not only to be forced by regulatory authorities. We can show that, if bank capital requirements were endogenous responses to the scrutiny of market players, a policy of low interest rates may restrict the banks' credibility.

This paper utilizes a simple overlapping principal-agent-style model of corporate finance which is in spirit of *Holmstrom* and *Tirole* (1997) and *Repullo* and *Suarez* (2000) and presents a simplified version of the model in *Dietrich* (2003). Basically, the model is dedicated to study the monetary policy transmission mechanism by combining arguments of the so called *broad credit channel* (*Oliner* and *Rudebusch* 1996) and of the *bank lending channel* (*Kashyap* and *Stein* 1994) by taking into account that banks have to be provided with incentives to monitor entrepreneurs. We argue that stipulating banks to possess some amount of own capital generate these incentives. We denote this capital requirement to be market based and show that this requirement depends crucially on interest rates and the cost of monitoring. After revealing some shortcomings of the credit crunch hypothesis, we apply this approach to the Japanese economy. As a result, a policy of very low interest rates may not only be inefficient but counterproductive to reactivate a stumbled economy.

2. A Model of External Finance

We consider an economy with many risk neutral entrepreneurs. Each entrepreneur runs a firm and possesses a risky investment opportunity (project) but is endowed with no own funds. The project costs 1 Yen in $T = 0$ and yields a return of either zero (in case of failure) or $R > 1$ (in case of success) in $T = 1$. The alternative return of a riskless investment opportunity is denoted by $\gamma > 1$, which is set by the monetary authority. Investors are risk neutral, small and competitive.

The probability of success $p \in [0;1]$ depends on the effort of the entrepreneur. We assume that the private cost of effort associated with p is given by:[4]

$$(1) \qquad\qquad f(p) = -p - \ln(1-p).$$

The entrepreneur and the investors agree on a financial contract that specifies the amount of external funds and the face value of the entrepreneur's debt (including principal and interest) to be paid to investors in case of success. Because of the

---

[4] We use this function for convenience only. Our results hold for any twice continuously differentiable, convex and increasing function satisfying $f'(0) = 0$ and $f'(1) = \infty$.

entrepreneur's limited liability, this repayment obligation H cannot exceed R. The investors are willing to provide funds if:

$$(2) \qquad\qquad pH = \gamma.$$

Owing to asymmetric information, the financial relationship between entrepreneur and investors suffers, however, from moral hazard. Hence, the probability of success p^{sb} chosen by the entrepreneur (second best) is such that it maximizes his net benefits $p(R-H)-f(p)$, i.e.:

$$(3) \qquad\qquad p^{sb} = \frac{R-H}{R-H+1}.$$

It follows:

$$(4) \qquad\qquad \frac{\partial p^{sb}}{\partial H} = -\frac{1}{(R-H+1)^2} < 0, \quad \frac{\partial^2 p^{sb}}{\partial H^2} = -\frac{2}{(R-H+1)^3} < 0.$$

Thus, an increasing repayment obligation worsens the incentives for the entrepreneur and this adverse incentive effect is the stronger the higher the repayment obligation is.

Denote the expected repayments to investors as $V := pH$ and assume $R > \gamma + 2\gamma^{1/2}$, i.e. the return in case of success is sufficiently large, we have:[5]

$$(5) \qquad\qquad \frac{\partial V}{\partial H} = \frac{R-H}{R-H+1} - \frac{H}{(R-H+1)^2} > 0, \quad \frac{\partial^2 V}{\partial H^2} = -2\frac{R+1}{(R-H+1)^3} < 0.$$

Thus, expected repayments V are an increasing but concave function of H, so that the entrepreneur and the investors agree upon the smallest repayment obligation that fulfills the reservation constraint of investors (2) subject to the incentive constraint (3). (If the return in case of success was smaller, the entrepreneur would be subject to credit rationing.)

To summarize, the optimum financial contract in case of direct finance follows from:

---

[5]   The proof is given in *Dietrich* (2003).

(6)
$$\max_{H} p(R-H) - f(p) \quad s.\ t. \quad (2),(3).$$

Next, consider bank loans as an alternative source of external finance. In a first step, we do not take into account the additional incentive constraint between bank and investors which results from asymmetric information between these parties. We assume that the bank is endowed with a monitoring technology, which provides perfect information on the effort chosen by the entrepreneur. Hence, there is no moral hazard at the entrepreneurial level. However, acquiring information is costly since it requires specific skills of a banker to monitor the entrepreneur. Denote this cost of monitoring by C.

Because monitoring eliminates moral hazard, the probability of success p^m in case of a bank loan contract maximizes the expected gains from trade $pR - f(p) - \gamma - C$:

(7)
$$p^m = \frac{R}{R+1} > p^{sb}.$$

Since p^m does not depend on H the repayment obligation H^m satisfies $p^m H^m = \gamma + C$, i.e.:

(8)
$$H^m = \frac{(\gamma + C)(R+1)}{R}.$$

However, monitoring the entrepreneur is efficient if and only if the associated net benefits of the entrepreneur are at least as high as in the case of direct external finance:

(9)
$$C \leq (p^m - p^{sb})R - [f(p^m) - f(p^{sb})],$$

otherwise the monitoring technology is too costly.

So far, we have assumed that the banker monitors the entrepreneur. However, owing to asymmetric information the investors cannot observe whether the banker will actually do so. One way to cope with this incentive problem is the *Diamond* (1984) principle assuming that loan risks are perfectly uncorrelated. In that case, a banker can credibly commit to monitor if she diversifies her loan portfolio perfectly. However, once perfect diversification is not possible (e.g., because of high systemic risks in a period of an economic recession) the *Diamond* (1984) principle does not work. Therefore, we follow *Holmstrom* and *Tirole* (1997) and ask whether a banker possesses sufficient own wealth or bank capital to be a credible monitor.

To proceed, we assume the following sequence of moves in the intermediation game:

1. The investors and the banker agree on a contract, which specifies the amount of funds provided by the investors and the face value of bank deposits owed to the investors.

2. The banker and the entrepreneur agree on a monitoring contract if condition (9) holds, i.e., if monitoring is not too costly (otherwise, the entrepreneur prefers direct finance without monitoring).

3. The banker decides whether to monitor the entrepreneur or not.

4. The entrepreneur provides an effort level associated with p^m if the banker monitors. Otherwise, he chooses a probability of success, which maximizes his expected net benefits with respect to the agreed-upon repayment obligation H^m.

We solve this overlapping moral hazard problem recursively. If the banker monitors, the entrepreneur performs the effort associated with p^m and the banker's expected rewards are $W = p^m (H - D)$ where D denotes the face value of deposits owed to investors. If the banker refuses to monitor the entrepreneur, the latter chooses an effort to maximize his net benefits subject to the repayment obligation H^m agreed upon in the bank loan contract. Denote the associated probability by p^{tb} which is given by:

(10)
$$p^{tb} = \frac{R - H^m}{R - H^m + 1}.$$

Because p^{tb} is smaller than p^m for all $H^m > 0$, expected rewards for a dishonest banker are also smaller than those for an honest. Consequently, the banker prefers monitoring if she is not worse off by doing so, i.e. if:

(11)
$$C \le (p^m - p^{tb})(H^m - D).$$

In our setting, since p^m and H^m are given by (7) and (8) respectively while p^{tb} follows from (10), there is a D^* satisfying (11) with equality for a given C. Hence, in order to provide the banker with the incentives to monitor an entrepreneur she has to share the credit risk sufficiently.

We follow *Holmstrom* and *Tirole* (1997) assuming that the banking industry is perfectly competitive. This implies that the banker has to invest own funds, say bank capital, such that the expected rewards associated with monitoring just cover the sum of the monitoring costs and the opportunity costs of these funds. From the participation constraint of investors it follows that investors are willing to provide funds amounting to at most $p^m D^* / \gamma$, and the banker has to possess at least:

(12) $$B_{crit} := \frac{p^{tb}}{\gamma}(H^m - D^*).$$

This condition is a main result of the analysis. A banker is credible to monitor if she is able to fund at least a specific endogenous fraction of her loans with own capital. If the banker fulfills this requirement, she will never try to cheat since her expected rewards do not outweigh the opportunity costs of provided own funds. Note, this capital requirement is market based, that is, investors will not be willing to invest their money in a bank, which cannot meet this requirement. If they would do so, the investors would have to expect that the banker will not monitor the entrepreneur and that her expected loan earnings are too small to meet investors' claims.

However, it is not generally warranted that the banker can promise a positive face value of deposits. If the maximum face value of deposits D^* just satisfying (11) is less than zero, the banker is not credible to monitor an entrepreneur even if she provides the entire amount of funds needed by the entrepreneur. The maximum face value of deposits is positive if and only if the cost of monitoring is not too large. The intuition behind this argument is as follows: Suppose that monitoring is costless, i.e. $C = 0$. In that case, the repayment obligation of the entrepreneur equals $H^m = \gamma(R+1)/R$. If the bank does not monitor, however, the entrepreneur realizes a probability of success p^{tb}, which is smaller than p^m. Therefore, the entrepreneur's expected repayments $p^{tb} H^m$ are smaller than γ. If, however, expected repayments to a dishonest bank were smaller than the opportunity cost of funds then the bank has an incentive to monitor. More formally, rearranging (11) yields:

(13) $$p^m H^m + (p^{tb} - p^m)D - C \geq p^{tb} H^m.$$

If $C = 0$, we have $p^m H^m = \gamma > p^{tb} H^m$ and therefore there exists a positive D^* for which (11) holds with equality. With increasing cost of monitoring the difference between $p^m H^m$ and C does not change because H^m is set according to (8), i.e., we have $\partial H^m / \partial C = 1/ p^m$. This implies, that $p^{tb} H^m$ is increasing in C, thus the right hand side of (13) increases. In order to meet the incentive constraint of the bank the face value of deposits D^* must decrease since $D^* < H^m$. Finally, if the cost of monitoring is too large there is no positive D^* which fulfills (11).

Now, we briefly discuss the properties of B_{crit}. First, and from the discussion above, the minimum capital position of a bank is increasing in the cost of monitoring:

Increasing monitoring cost raises a banker's opportunity cost of being honest, thus a banker has to share a higher proportion of the credit risk, i.e., she has to meet a higher capital requirement to signal credibility. Second, the capital requirement of a bank depends on the alternative return γ of the riskless investment:

$$(14) \qquad \frac{\partial B_{crit}}{\partial \gamma} = -\frac{B_{crit}}{\gamma} + \frac{(H^m - D^*)}{\gamma} \frac{\partial p^{tb}}{\partial \gamma} + \frac{p^{tb}}{\gamma} \left(\frac{\partial H^m}{\partial \gamma} - \frac{\partial D^*}{\partial \gamma} \right) < 0.$$

Increasing interest rates raise the opportunity cost of bank's invested funds. Thus, a banker's opportunity cost of being diligently decreases. Second, a rising γ implies that the repayment obligation H^m increases to meet the investors' reservation constraint. However, this makes the entrepreneur even lazier in the case of no monitoring, i.e., p^{tb} decreases, and therefore expected rewards of a dishonest banker decrease as well. This makes the banker even more credible and her capital requirement decreases. Third, the repayment obligation H^m and the face value of deposits D^* change after a variation in interest rates. *Dietrich* (2003) shows that, after all, the sign of $\partial B_{crit} / \partial \gamma$ is strictly negative.

3. The Effects of Monetary Policy

After developing a small framework for analyzing market based capital requirements for banks, we first refer to the arguments of the capital crunch literature concerning the Japanese puzzle. Because of the regulatory capital requirements proposed by the *Basle Committee* in 1988 and implemented definitively by the Japanese government in March 1993, Japanese internationally operating banks must hold bank capital positions to be equal to at least 8 % of total risk-weighted assets. Without detailing the institutional framework of the *Basle Accord*, it is important to note the different treatment of loans to member states of *OECD*, their central banks and loans backed by them on the one hand and loans to nonbanks on the other hand. The former are not subject to capital requirements because of risk-weighting coefficients equal to zero whereas the latter have risk-weighted coefficients of either *0.5* or *1.0* depending on the nature of the lending operation (see *Dewatripont* and *Tirole* 1994). Hence, according to the capital crunch hypothesis, a bank with a poor capital position has to reallocate its portfolio in favor of safe claims on treasury accounts while curtailing bank lending to firms even in periods of a loose monetary policy in order to meet regulatory capital requirements.

In Japan, banks suffered from a dramatic shortage of capital because of a busted asset price bubble. Although monetary policy attempting to reactivate the Japanese economy with low interest rates has resulted in a more or less steady growth of money, bank lending of domestic commercial banks has declined by an annual rate of nearly 2 % on average since 1997 (Figure 1). However, there is a striking feature of the Japanese banking industry in the late 1990s, which suggests that the capital crunch hypothesis is only half of the story because, at present, the Japanese banking industry is much healthier ever since the end of the golden decade. Banks that were in trouble in 1997 as for example the *Long Term Credit Bank of Japan* were recapitalized by the Japanese government, which injected more than Yen 60 trillion of public funds into the banking sector in 1998 in order to recapitalize banks (*Hoshi* 2001). As a result, all the major banks meet the *Basle* capital requirement with capital-asset-ratios of more than 10 %. Note that without public funds injected in the banking industry the average capital-asset-ratio of all banks would have been around 8.5 % (*Hoggarth* and *Thomas* 1999).

Figure 1:   Bank lending by domestic commercial banks

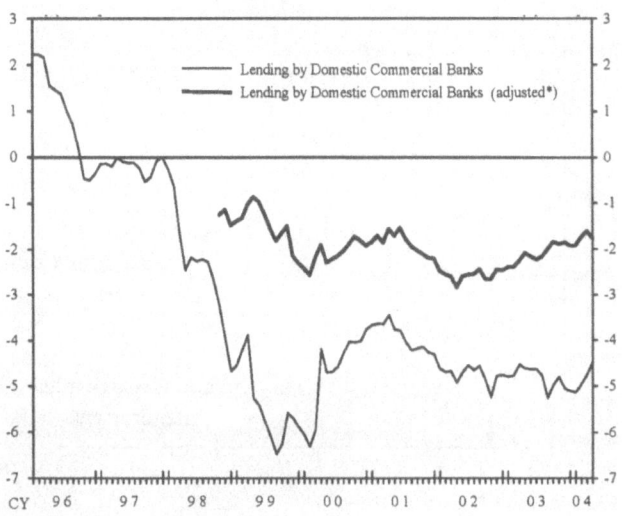

Note: Percent changes in average amounts outstanding from a year earlier.
       *) Adjusted to exclude 1) fluctuations due to the liquidation of loans and loan write-offs, 2) fluctuations in the yen value of foreign-currency denominated loans, 3) the transfer of loans to governmental corporations.

Source: *Bank of Japan* (2004).

However, "...there is speculation in the private sector that the funds available for recapitalization are still insufficient to allow banks to increase lending significantly" (*Hoggarth* and *Thomas* 1999, p. 87). The influence of these market based capital requirements on the efficacy of monetary policy can be studied in the framework outlined here. According to equation (14), we have an inverse correlation between interest rates and the bank capital requirement resulting from market scrutiny. If interest rates are very low it is possible that market based capital requirements are stronger than regulatory capital requirements. In that case, the former are binding, and a loose monetary policy with a further decrease of interest rates hurts the market players' confidence in the banking sector even more.

Figure 2 illustrates this argument. If interest rates are relatively high, the regulatory capital requirement with a capital-asset-ratio of 8 % is binding. In that case the capital crunch argument holds, i.e., if banks just meet this requirement but have no excess capital positions (as in point Y for example), a monetary easing does not lead to an increase in bank lending but only to an increase in treasury claims. This is because the latter require no additional bank capital due to regulatory risk-weighting coefficients equal to zero.

Figure 2:   **Market based capital requirements versus regulatory capital requirements**

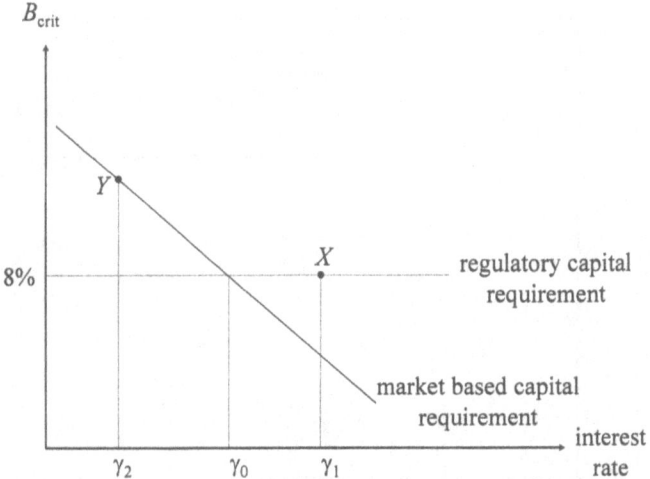

However, if interest rates are low, capital requirements resulting from market scrutiny are binding, and banks have to fulfill even higher requirements if interest rates further decrease as in Japan (see Figure 3). This is because bank´s opportunity cost of being diligently is relatively high and increasing with falling interest rates. The situation represented by point X in Figure 2 can be viewed as a possible explanation of the Japanese puzzle. Because of binding capital requirements due to market scrutiny, decreasing interest rates tighten the credibility problem of banks so that banks have to restrict bank lending for a given amount of bank capital in order to meet market based capital requirements.

This hypothesis is mainly supported by three empirical findings. First, the actual capital position of Japanese banks is in excess regarding the regulatory capital requirements of the *Basle Accord*. Therefore, the regulatory capital requirements do not constrain bank lending. As a second observation, although the money stock increases the volume of bank lending is declining. This pattern cannot be explained by the capital crunch hypothesis because this would require at least constant bank lending. The third finding concerns the empirical correlation between actual bank capital and bank lending activities. For the early 1990s, bank lending seems not to be constrained by banks' actual capital positions as the study of *Woo* (1999) suggests. However, *Woo* (1999) also shows in a cross-sectional regression analysis that after 1995 a break with this pattern occurs and bank lending depends significantly on bank capital. This observation implies that capital requirements became binding in 1995-96, i.e., since interest rates have been very low.

Figure 3:   Government bond yield (10-year) in percent.

Source: *Bank of Japan* (2004).

4. Discussion

The objective of the paper was to study the interactions of a bank's capital position and the efficacy of monetary policy with zero interest rates in Japan. The main result of the analysis is that banks have to meet even higher capital requirements in order to signal credibility to market players if interest rates are very low. In that case, a monetary policy of decreasing interest rates forces banks to reallocate their loan portfolios in favor of claims on treasury accounts, i.e., bank lending decreases and banks use additional liquidity provided by the central bank to purchase treasury bills.

How can the Bank of Japan escape from that precarious situation? As argued here, a policy of low interest rates alone may have an adverse effect on one possible channel of monetary policy transmission. However, there are still other ways of affecting the real economy. A straightforward way to stimulate the Japanese economy is to foster real money growth. Beyond traditional interest rate cuts and providing liquidity to banks, the central bank can do so by open market operations buying other assets, e.g., corporate bonds, government bonds, or even foreign exchange (*McCallum* 2000). In either way, asset yields have to adjust to balance money demand and supply and thereby raising aggregate demand (*Meltzer* 2001). Once the economy has recovered, interest rates increase and banks regain credibility to monitor borrowers. Secondly, a restructuring of the stumbled financial system in Japan is due (*Hoshi* and *Kashyap* 2004). The main objective of restructuring must be to provide banks with incentives to control their credit risks actively (even in periods of low interest rates) accepting that some banks, perhaps some large banks, do not survive the restructuring process. That way also allows new healthy banks to emerge, which will later on extend lending to the private sector (*Caballero, Hoshi* and *Kashyap* 2003).

References

Bank of Japan (2004), Monthly Report of Recent Economic and Financial Developments, Tokyo, May.

Bernanke, B. S. and *C. S. Lown* (1991), The Credit Crunch, in: Brookings Papers on Economic Activity, Vol. 2, pp. 205-239.

Bolton, P. and *X. Freixas* (2001), Corporate Finance and the Monetary Transmission Mechanism, CEPR Discussion Paper No. 2892, London.

Caballero, R.; T. Hoshi and *A. Kashyap* (2003), Zombie Lending and Depressed Restructuring in Japan, University of Chicago Working Paper.

Calomiris, C. W. (1999), Building an Incentive-compatible Safety Net, in: Journal of Banking and Finance, Vol. 23, pp. 1499-1519.

Calomiris, C. W. and *C. M. Kahn* (1991), The Role of Demandable Debt in Structuring Optimal Banking Arrangements, in: American Economic Review, Vol. 81, pp. 497-513.

Dewatripont, M. and *J. Tirole* (1994), The Prudential Regulation of Banks, Cambridge MA.

Diamond, D. W. (1984), Financial Intermediation and Delegated Monitoring, in: Review of Economic Studies, Vol. 51, pp. 393-414.

Diamond, D. W. (2001), Should Japanese Banks be Recapitalized?, in: *Bank of Japan*, Monetary and Economic Studies, Vol. 19, No. 2, pp. 1-19.

Dietrich, D. (2003), Monetary Policy Shocks and Heterogeneous Finance Decisions: A model of Hidden Effort Choice and Financial Intermediation, in: German Economic Review, Vol. 4, pp. 365-388.

Herring, R. J. and *S. Wachter* (1999), Real Estate Booms and Banking Busts: An International Perspective. The Wharton Financial Institutions Center Working Paper, No. 99-27.

Hoggarth, G. and *J. Thomas* (1999), Will Bank Recapitalisation Boost Domestic Demand in Japan?, Bank of England Financial Stability Review, pp. 85-93.

Holmstrom, B. and *J. Tirole* (1997), Financial Intermediation, Loanable Funds, and the Real Sector, in: Quarterly Journal of Economics, Vol. 112, pp. 663-691.

Hoshi, T. (2001), What Happened to Japanese Banks?, in: Bank of Japan, Monetary and Economic Studies, Vol. 19(1), pp. 1-28.

Hoshi, T. and *A. Kashyap* (2000), The Japanese Banking Crisis: Where Did it Come From and How Will it End?, NBER Macroeconomics Annual, NBER, Cambridge MA, pp. 129-201.

Hoshi, T. and *A. Kashyap* (2004), Japan's Financial Crisis and Economic Stagnation, in: Journal of Economic Perspectives, Vol. 18, pp. 3-26.

Kanaya, A. and *D. Woo* (2000), The Japanese Banking Crisis of the 1990s: Sources and Lessons, IMF Working Paper WP/00/7.

Kashyap, A. K. and *J. C. Stein* (1994), Monetary Policy and Bank Lending, in: *N. G. Mankiw* (ed.), Monetary Policy. NBER Studies in Business Cycles, Vol. 29, NBER, Chicago, pp. 221-261.

Krugman, P. (1998), It's baaack: Japan's Slump and the Return of Liquidity Trap, in: Brookings Papers on Economic Activity, Vol. 2, pp. 137-205.

McCallum, B. T. (2000), Theoretical Analysis Regarding a Zero Lower Bound on Nominal Interest Rates, in: Journal of Money, Credit, and Banking, Vol. 32, pp. 870-904.

McKinnon, R. I. (2000), The Foreign Exchange Origins of Japan's Liquidity Trap, in: Cato Journal, Vol. 20, pp. 73-84.

Meltzer, A. H. (2000), Monetary Policy in the New Global Economy: The Case of Japan, in: Cato Journal, Vol. 20, pp. 69-72.

Meltzer, A. H. (2001), The Transmission Process, in: *Deutsche Bundesbank* (ed.), The Monetary Transmission Process, Hampshire, New York, pp. 112-130.

Okina, K. (1999), Monetary Policy under Zero Inflation: A Response to Criticism and Questions Regarding Monetary Policy, in: *Bank of Japan*, Monetary and Economic Studies, Vol. 17, No. 3, pp. 157-182.

Oliner, S. D. and *G. D. Rudebusch* (1996), Is There a Broad Credit Channel for Monetary Policy?, in: Federal Reserve Bank of San Francisco Economic Review, Vol. 1, pp. 3-13.

Repullo, R. and *J. Suarez* (2000), Entrepreneurial Moral Hazard and Bank Monitoring: A Model of the Credit Channel, in: European Economic Review, Vol. 44, pp. 1931-1950.

Woo, D. (1999), In Search of "Capital Crunch": Supply Factors Behind the Credit Slowdown in Japan, IMF Working Paper WP/99/3.

Rolf Hasse und Uwe Vollmer (eds.)
Incentives and Economic Behaviour
Schriften zu Ordnungsfragen der Wirtschaft · Band 76 · Stuttgart · 2005

Intrinsische Motivation und Delegation

Silvia Föhr und *Harald Wiese*

Inhalt

1. Einführung

In typischen Arbeitsbeziehungen geht man davon aus, dass eine Hierarchie von Entscheidungsträgern existiert. Es gibt mindestens einen „Chef" - den Prinzipal - und mindestens einen Mitarbeiter - den Agenten -, der im Auftrag des Vorgesetzten Aufgaben ausführt und dabei ein bestimmtes Arbeitsergebnis erzielt. In Mehrpersonen-unternehmen wirken Agenten aufgrund der Hoffnung auf Synergieeffekte bzw. Kooperationsrenten zusammen, die jedoch durch das so genannte „Freifahrerproblem" aufgrund asymmetrisch verteilter Informationen und Unsicherheit gefährdet werden können. Die Überwachung der Agenten und/oder die Installierung von Anreizsystemen wird dann notwendig. Zur Analyse solcher Überwachungs- und Anreizsysteme wird die Prinzipal-Agenten-Theorie herangezogen.

Im Grundmodell dieser Theorie leistet ein Agent mehr oder weniger große Anstrengung im Sinne der Ziele des Prinzipals. Der Prinzipal interveniert typischerweise durch eine Mischung von Kontrollen und Anreizen. Man formuliert das Prinzipal-Agenten-Problem als ein Optimierungsproblem des Prinzipals unter mindestens zwei Nebenbedingungen. Die erste Nebenbedingung ist die Teilnahmebedingung (participation constraint) des Agenten. Er erwartet aus der Beschäftigung einen Nutzen, der mindestens so hoch wie sein exogen vorgegebener Reservationsnutzen ist. Wenn der Agent sich zur Teilnahme entschließt, so hat er die Wahl zwischen mehreren Handlungen. Die vom Prinzipal angestrebte Handlung sollte dem Agenten mindestens so viel erwarteten Nutzen bringen wie jede andere mögliche Handlung. Diese zweite Nebenbedingung wird Anreizkompatibilität (incentive compatibility) genannt.

Typischerweise wird in diesen Modellen davon ausgegangen, dass der Prinzipal risikoneutral und der Agent risikoscheu ist. Aus Gründen der Risikoaufteilung wäre ein fester Lohn, der nicht von unsicheren Ergebnissen der Handlung des Agenten abhängt, optimal. Im Hinblick auf die Anreizkompatibilität möchte der Prinzipal bei asymmetrischer Information über die Handlung des Agenten diesen jedoch am Erfolg und somit auch am Risiko beteiligen. In diesen Modellen führt eine verstärkte Kontrolle des Agenten durch den Prinzipal und/oder eine stärkere Belohnung für zielkonformes Verhalten (bzw. Bestrafung für Verhalten gegen die Interessen des Prinzipals) dazu, dass der Agent sich eher konform zu den Zielen des Prinzipals verhält. Dieses Ergebnis kann als die Monotonie der externen Intervention bezeichnet werden. Insoweit als die Überwachung des Agenten dem Prinzipal Kosten oder als Ungleichheit der Entlohnung dem Agenten Kosten verursacht, hat man es jedoch mit einem nichttrivialen Optimierungsproblem zu tun; es kann überoptimale Intervention geben.

In diesem Beitrag wird ein kurzer Überblick gegeben, wie Mitarbeiter zur Verfolgung organisatorischer Ziele zu motivieren sind. Dazu wird zunächst auf die „klassischen" Motivationstheorien eingegangen, in denen neben den für die Prinzipal-Agenten-Theorie typischen, extrinsischen (monetären) Anreizen die Bedeutung von intrinsischen Anreizen hervorgehoben wird. Weitere Aufsätze, die etwas vertiefter diskutiert werden sollen, gehen genauer auf das Wechselspiel zwischen intrinsischen und extrinsischen Anreizen ein. Die Beiträge nehmen Bezug auf die Prinzipal-Agenten-Theorie und stellen unabhängig voneinander die Monotoniethese in Frage. *Frey* (1997) sowie *Frey* und *Jegen* (2001) kritisieren, dass Prinzipal-Agenten-Modelle nur extrinsische Motivation, nicht jedoch intrinsische Motivation berücksichtigen. *Frey* betont insbesondere die Gefahr, dass Interventionen der Prinzipale (die Installation von Überwachungs- und Anreizsystemen) die intrinsische Motivation „verdrängen" könnten (so genanntes „crowding out"). Die traditionelle Prinzipal-Agenten-Analyse vernach-lässigt nach *Frey* diesen wichtigen Aspekt. Man kann nun das Initiativmodell von *Aghion* und *Tirole* (1997) und weitere Beiträge, z.B. *Kunz* und *Pfaff* (2002), *Murdock* (2002) und *Bénabou* und *Tirole* (2003), als eine Manifestation dieser Verdrängung intrinsischer Motivation verstehen. In diesem Beitrag wird schließlich eine erweiterte Variante des Initiativmodells vorgestellt, die Verdrängungseffekte hierin identifiziert und darüber hinaus verdeutlicht, wie verschiedene Formen intrinsischer Motivation formal modelliert werden könnten.

2. Extrinsische und intrinsische Motivation - ein Überblick

Argyris (1990) stellt im Rückblick auf jahrzehntelange Motivationsforschung die Hypothese auf, dass der Mensch im Wesentlichen intrinsisch motiviert und kontrolliert ist. Externe, d.h. von Seiten der Organisation eingerichtete und auferlegte Be- und Entlohnungssysteme und Kontrollmechanismen sind eher dazu geeignet, die individuelle Persönlichkeit in ihrer Entwicklung einzuengen und sie zu einer Anpassungshaltung zu veranlassen, die einen qualitativ niedrigen Grad an Maturiertheit (= geistig-seelischer Reifungs- und Entwicklungsstand) impliziert (nach *Weinert* 1998, S. 562). Auch wenn diese Sichtweise zu streng erscheint, gibt sie den Ökonomen den impliziten „Auftrag", in ihren Modellen auch intrinsische Anreizfaktoren zu berücksichtigen. Bevor dies mit Hilfe des erweiterten Modells von *Aghion* und *Tirole* (1997) geschehen soll, werden in einem Überblick Grundgedanken von relevanten Motivationstheorien skizziert. Ziel dieser knappen Einführung ist zu zeigen, welche Inhalte mit extrinsischer und intrinsischer Motivation verbunden werden, wie und in welchem Ausmaß Motivationsfaktoren wirken und ob die Erkenntnisse gestalterisch umzusetzen sind.

In der Motivationsforschung wird nach den Gründen für menschliches Verhalten und Erleben gesucht. Motivation erklärt einerseits beobachtbares Verhalten, für das bestimmte Motive unterstellt werden. Andererseits ist „Motivation" aber auch der Begriff für direktes Erleben, das für die theoretische Analyse abstrahiert werden muss. Motiviertes Verhalten folgt in der Theorie einem konkreten Ablauf: Nach der Erfahrung eines Mangels wird eine Erwartung darüber gebildet, dass durch ein spezifisches Verhalten der Mangel beseitigt wird. Das Verhalten wird in der Annahme, dass es der Beseitigung des Mangels dient, ausgewählt und schließlich in einer Endhandlung ausgeführt. Nicht automatisch gewährleistet ist die dauerhafte Mangelbeseitigung, so dass es zu einem Schwanken zwischen Mangel und Sättigung kommt. Motive können zudem nach Defizit- und Wachstumsmotiven unterschieden werden. Erstere gleichen

Regelkreisen, die bei Abweichungen vom Sollwert eine Wiederherstellung des Ausgangszustandes durch entsprechende Aktivitäten bewirken. Bei Wachstumsmotiven verändern sich ständig die Zielsetzungen und damit auch die Sollwerte. Mit einer gewissen Dynamik verändern sich Anspruchsniveaus und Instrumente (vgl. z.B. *Rosenstiel* 1993).

In den Motivationstheorien wird auch untersucht, was und welche Faktoren den Menschen zur Arbeit motivieren. Im Wesentlichen geht es dabei um Bedürfnisse und die Be- und Entlohnungen, die zum bestimmten Verhalten anreizen. Aufbauend auf den „Klassikern", wie z.B. der *Maslow'* schen Bedürfnispyramide oder der Zwei-Faktoren-Theorie von *Herzberg* (1966), die Motivationsfaktoren (z.B. Leistung, Anerkennung, Verantwortung) und Hygienefaktoren (z.B. Bezahlung, Arbeitsplatzsicherheit, Status, organisatorische Regelwerke) unterscheidet, werden in späteren, ganz unterschiedlichen Theorierichtungen die extrinsische und intrinsische Motivation differenziert. Im Zentrum des Interesses steht dabei die Deutung, wie menschliches Verhalten ausgelöst und verändert werden kann. Wenn – wie z.B. in den *Prozesstheorien* unterstellt – Menschen sich kognitiv mit einem gewünschten Ergebnis als Ziel auseinandersetzen und dieses mit einem möglichst geringen Mitteleinsatz erreichen wollen, kann von einer Instrumentalität ausgegangen werden, d.h. ein Handelnder geht instrumentell vor, um ein bestimmtes Ergebnis (z.B. Zufriedenheit, Nutzen) zu erreichen. Prominentester Ansatz ist hier die Erwartungs-Valenz-Theorie von *Vroom* (1964), in der vertreten wird, dass die Arbeitsleistung von der Motivation und der Fähigkeit des Mitarbeiters abhängt. Die Motivation kann auch als Bemühung, ein bestimmtes Ergebnis zu erreichen, verstanden werden. Die Bedeutung des Endergebnisses für den Mitarbeiter hängt zudem von seiner subjektiven Einschätzung der Wahrscheinlichkeit ab, dieses Ergebnis auch zu erreichen. Mitarbeiter bilden also Erwartungen darüber, ob das Bemühen zu einer hohen Arbeitsleistung führt und ob das Handeln tatsächlich zu einem konkreten Ergebnis (Beförderung, Lohnerhöhung, Belobigung usw.) führt, und bewerten gleichzeitig, wie wichtig das Endergebnis für sie selbst ist. Extrinsische und intrinsische Motivatoren fließen hier gleichermaßen ein. In einem anderen Ansatz von *Porter* und *Lawler* (1968) wird der Zusammenhang zwischen Arbeitsleistung und dem Ergebnis des Arbeitsprozesses, der Arbeitszufriedenheit, noch deutlicher hergestellt. Auch hier spielen subjektive Wahrscheinlichkeiten für den Erfolg der Bemühungen, ein Ziel zu erreichen, und dafür, dass dieses erreichte Ziel dann auch zufrieden stellt, eine erhebliche Rolle. Über eine Selbstevaluation wird ein Grad an Zufriedenheit erreicht, der den Unterschied zwischen Erwartung und Zustand einer Belohnung markiert (vgl. zu einer kritischen Position *Weinert* 1998).

In Arbeitsbeziehungen wird von *intrinsischer* Motivation gesprochen, wenn die Motivation ihre Befriedigung in der Arbeitsaufgabe selbst findet. Inhalte intrinsischer Motivatoren können die Möglichkeit zur Autonomie, Vielseitigkeit der Aufgaben, positive Rückkopplung oder erkennbare Bedeutung von Arbeitsinhalten sein. *Extrinsische* Anreize ermöglichen eine Befriedigung der Bedürfnisse als Mittel zum Zweck. Neben dem Geld gehören z.B. Karriereoptionen oder Statussymbole zu den extrinsischen Anreizen. Typischerweise wird davon ausgegangen, dass für eine Gestaltung von Anreizen eine Abstimmung von Anreizprofilen mit Bedürfnisprofilen zu beachten ist. Erst der „Fit" zwischen Anreizen und Bedürfnissen kann in der Organisation zu Erfolgen führen, wobei meist von der Komplementarität einzelner Anreize, also auch von extrinsischen und intrinsischen, ausgegangen wird (z.B. *Schanz* 1991, S. 25). Für die Gestaltung motivierender Situationen wird u.a. unterstellt, dass der Vorgesetzte mit seinem Führungsverhalten eine starke Rolle in der intrinsischen Motivation spielt. Zudem ist die Gestaltung der Arbeitsaufgabe eine der wichtigsten Einflussvariablen für die Arbeitszufriedenheit, was insbesondere für den möglichst großen, aber noch zu bewältigenden Handlungsspielraum und für die Delegation gilt (*Rosenstiel* 1993, S. 169). Hinsichtlich der Höhe der Bezahlung vermutet *Rosenstiel* (1993, S. 170), dass sie nicht direkt positiv mit der Zufriedenheit korreliert, sondern dass die Anreizwirkung zum einen von anderen Belohnungsformen (z.B. Ansehen, Handlungsspielräume) und zum anderen von einem sozialen Kontext bzw. Vergleich abhängt. Einige empirische Untersuchungen können belegen, dass hohe intrinsische Motivation eher bei interessanten Aufgaben, bei Berufen mit Exzellenzstandards, bei persönlichen Beziehungen zwischen Prinzipal und Agent und bei extensiven Beteiligungsmöglichkeiten vorliegt (*Frey* 1997, S. 431f.).

3. Zur Verdrängung der intrinsischen durch die extrinsische Motivation

3.1. Die Verdrängungshypothese von *Frey*

Anders als die bisher genannten Autoren unterstellt *Frey* die Gefahr, dass intrinsische Motivation - aus der Arbeitsaufgabe und der daraus gespeisten Arbeitszufriedenheit - durch die Gewährung extrinsischer (positiver und negativer) Anreize verdrängt werden kann. *Frey* hat in einer Serie von Aufsätzen (u.a. 1993a, 1993b, 1997) sowie *Frey* und *Jegen* (2001) darauf hingewiesen, dass die ausschließliche Betonung so genannter extrinsischer Motivation zu Fehleinschätzungen bei der Installation von Kontroll- und Anreizsystemen führen kann.

Frey (1997), *Frey* und *Jegen* (2001) sowie *Frey* und *Osterloh* (1997) kritisieren vor allem die neoinstitutionalistischen Ansätze, allen voran die Prinzipal-Agenten-Theorie, die nur extrinsische Anreize modelliere. Sie behaupten im Gegenzug, dass die extrinsische Motivation intrinsische Motivation verdränge, und dass man als Prinzipal bei einer motivierenden Aufgabenstellung und Arbeitsgestaltung viel weniger extrinsische Anreize setzen müsse. Verdrängung intrinsischer Motivation ("crowding out" in *Frey* und *Jegen* 2001) drohe dabei insbesondere unter folgenden Umständen (siehe *Frey* 1997, S. 430 ff.):

– Anweisungen oder Belohnungen für spezifische Leistungen führen eher zur Verdrängung intrinsischer Motivation als generelle Anerkennung oder Belohnungen im Falle guter Ergebnisse.

- Agenten mit überdurchschnittlicher Arbeitsmoral fühlen sich durch gleichartige externe Intervention gegenüber allen Agenten missachtet und reduzieren ihre intrinsische Motivation.

- Nach der sozialpsychologischen Theorie der verborgenen Kosten der Belohnung von *Deci* und *Ryan* (1985) führt eine extrinsische Motivation bei Vorhandensein intrinsischer Motivation zur „Übermotivierung", die durch Abbau der intrinsischen Motivation reduziert wird.

Der Verdrängungseffekt besteht nach *Frey* und *Osterloh* (1997, S. 310 ff.) darin, dass (1.) Kontrolle und eine verminderte Selbstbestimmung in Verbindung mit der kognitiven Bewertung von Belohnungen motivationssenkend wirken können, während z.B. Kompetenzzuweisungen motivationssteigernd wirken. Außerdem wird angenommen, dass (2.) über einen impliziten Vertrag eine gegenseitige Wertschätzung der Vertragspartner erzeugt wird. Monetäre Belohnungen könnten dann gegen diesen impliziten Vertrag verstoßen und motivationsmindernd wirken. Dagegen spricht jedoch, dass (3.) eine geringere als die vereinbarte (monetäre) Belohnung aufgrund der empfundenen Unfairness ebenfalls zur Motivationsstörung führen kann. Geraten (4.) die Mitarbeiter unter Druck aufgrund der in Aussicht gestellten monetären Belohnungen bei vorher vereinbarter Leistung, kann freiwilliges Engagement der Mitarbeiter abnehmen. Einige dieser Überlegungen lassen sich jedoch auch in neoinstitutionalistischen Modellen durchführen. So werden wir später zeigen können, wie Kontrolle die Bemühungen um Eigeninitiative, z.B. bei der Informationsbeschaffung, verdrängen kann.

Der Verdienst *Freys* besteht darin, die Vertreter mikroökonomischer Modelle und insbesondere der Prinzipal-Agenten-Theorie an die Relevanz intrinsischer Motivation und der Gefahr der Verdrängung zu erinnern. Die Integration effizienz- und verhaltensorientierter Elemente ist in jüngster Zeit durch die Verhaltensökonomik („behavioral economics") erfolgreich begonnen worden. Mit empirischen Forschungsansätzen im Labor und im Feld wurde individuelles Verhalten in ökonomisch relevanten Entscheidungssituationen näher untersucht, und einige Vorschläge zur Implementierung ausgewählter Erkenntnisse in ökonomische Modelle sind entwickelt worden (vgl. u.a. *Fehr* und *Schmidt* 1999, *Fehr* und *Falk* 2002, *Rabin* 2002, *Tirole* 2002). *Frey* stellt im Beitrag mit *Jegen* aus dem Jahr 2001 eine Vielzahl von empirischen Befunden aus sowohl psychologischen als auch ökonomischen Labor- und Feldstudien zusammen, die zumindest Indizien für Crowding-Effekte beinhalten bzw. belegen „that strong empirical evidence indeed exists for crowding-out and crowding-in." (*Frey* and *Jegen* 2001, S. 606). *Kunz* und *Pfaff* (2002, S. 282 ff.) gehen sehr kritisch mit dem Konstrukt der intrinsischen Motivation um und relativieren die empirischen Befunde vor dem Hintergrund, dass die verborgenen Kosten der Belohnung ("hidden costs of reward") in Unternehmen aufgrund der Antizipation dieses Effekts durch organisatorische Maßnahmen leicht zu umgehen sind (*Kunz* und *Pfaff* 2002, S. 290 ff.).

In der Folge wird auf der reinen Modellebene gezeigt, dass die Motivationsforschung mit Hilfe von einfachen Prinzipal-Agenten-Ansätzen zu präzisieren und zumindest von der Richtung her zu quantifizieren ist. In diesem Sinne stellen wir in Abschnitt 3.2 das Modell von *Aghion* und *Tirole* (1997) vor, in dem die Verdrängung der Motivation des Agenten aufgrund verstärkter Kontrolle *endogen* hergeleitet wird. In eigenen Weiterentwicklungen dieses Modells führen wir außerdem intrinsische Motivatoren verschiedenster Art direkt in das Modell ein. Es bleibt aber zu beachten, dass mühsame Versuche, Quellen intrinsischer Motivation aufzuspüren und für die Gestaltung von Anreizsystemen einzusetzen, wiederum Organisationskosten verursachen, deren Deckung durch höhere individuelle Leistungen empirisch noch zu belegen ist.

3.2. Verdrängung von Initiative im Modell von *Aghion* und *Tirole*

Während typische Prinzipal-Agenten-Ansätze davon ausgehen, dass eine verstärkte Kontrolle des Agenten durch den Prinzipal und/oder eine höhere Belohnung für ein Verhalten im Interesse des Prinzipals den Agent veranlasst, sich eher konform zu den Zielen des Prinzipals zu verhalten, widerlegen *Aghion* and *Tirole* (1997) diese Monotonieannahme.

Die Autoren haben ein Modell entwickelt, innerhalb dessen sich die Monotoniethese nicht bestätigt. Sie zeigen, dass unter plausiblen Annahmen die Bereitschaft des Agenten, Informationen zu sammeln, von den Informationsaktivitäten des Prinzipals negativ beeinflusst wird. Die Verdrängung von Motivation wird hier ohne Rückgriff auf ad-hoc-Annahmen über intrinsische Motivation gezeigt.

In der einfachen Variante bei *Aghion* and *Tirole* (1997) untersucht der Agent für den Prinzipal die Durchführungsmöglichkeit von drei Projekten, die zu Auszahlungen π_P und π_A für den Prinzipal bzw. für den Agenten führen. Diese Auszahlungen umschließen für den Agenten Aspekte wie das Erwerben von Humankapital, die Möglichkeit, sein Können zu signalisieren und den Nutzen der Durchführung des Projektes. Projekt *0* ist der Status quo, mit Auszahlungen von $\pi_P^0 = \pi_A^0 = 0$ für den Prinzipal bzw. den Agenten. Projekt 1 erbringt für den Agenten $\pi_A^1 = 0$, während der Prinzipal sich mit $\pi_P^1 = \pi_P^{mx} > 0$ hierbei am besten stellt. Projekt 2 erbringt für den Agenten $\pi_A^2 = \pi_A^{mx} > 0$, während der Prinzipal lediglich $\pi_P^2 = \pi_P^{mn}$ mit $0 < \pi_P^{mn} < \pi_P^{mx}$ erhält.

Sowohl der Prinzipal als auch der Agent können nun unter Hinnahme von (Informations-) Kosten die Wahrscheinlichkeit beeinflussen, mit der sie die Auszahlungen der Projekte in Erfahrung bringen. Konkret sind $c_P(w_P)$ die Kosten für den Prinzipal, falls die Wahrscheinlichkeit dafür, dass er die Auszahlung der Projekte kennt, w_P betragen soll. Mit Wahrscheinlichkeit $1 - w_P$ erfährt der Prinzipal dann nichts über die Projekte und kann sie nicht unterscheiden. Analog bedeutet $c_A(w_A)$ die Kosten des Agenten, mit Wahrscheinlichkeit w_A die Auszahlungen der Projekte zu erfahren.

Vorausgesetzt wird, dass die Informationskostenfunktionen monoton steigend und streng konvex sind und obendrein $c_i(0) = c_i'(0) = 0$ und $c_i(1) = \infty$ für $i = P, A$ erfüllen. Diese Kostenfunktion bewirkt, dass sich ein wenig Informationssammeln immer lohnen wird und dass die Wahrscheinlichkeit *1* nie angestrebt wird.

Die zeitliche Abfolge des Modells ist diese:

1. Prinzipal und Agent treffen gleichzeitig die Informationsentscheidung und wenden dazu Kosten $c_P(w_P)$ und $c_A(w_A)$ auf.

2. Der Agent schlägt entweder den Status quo, d.h. Projekt *0* vor, oder, falls er sich informieren konnte, Projekt *2*, das die Auszahlungen (π_A^{mx}, π_P^{mn}) erbringt.

3. Falls der Prinzipal sich nicht informiert hat, bleibt ihm nichts anderes übrig, als den Vorschlag zu akzeptieren. Anderenfalls setzt er sich mit seinem Vorschlag (Projekt *1*) durch, was zu Auszahlungen $(0, \pi_P^{mx})$ führt.

Man kann die Ergebnisse der zweiten und dritten Stufe in die Nutzenfunktionen integrieren, die dann lediglich von den gewählten Wahrscheinlichkeiten w_P und w_A abhängen. Man erhält für den Prinzipal:

$$u_P = \underbrace{w_P \pi_P^{mx}}_{\substack{\text{Prinzipal ist} \\ \text{informiert}}} + \underbrace{(1 - w_P) w_A \pi_P^{mn}}_{\substack{\text{Prinzipal ist nicht informiert,} \\ \text{Agent ist informiert}}} - c_P(w_P)$$

und für den Agenten:

$$u_A = \underbrace{w_P \cdot 0}_{\substack{\text{Prinzipal ist} \\ \text{informiert}}} + \underbrace{(1 - w_P) w_A \pi_A^{mx}}_{\substack{\text{Prinzipal ist nicht informiert,} \\ \text{Agent ist informiert}}} - c_A(w_A).$$

Man sieht, dass es im Interesse des Prinzipals ist, wenn sich der Agent um Informationen bemüht. Umgekehrt ist es für den Agenten vorteilhaft, wenn sich der Prinzipal nicht informiert. Um das Gleichgewicht zu bestimmen, werden zunächst die Grenznutzen der Beteiligten berechnet. Sie lauten:

$$\frac{du_P}{dw_P} = \underbrace{\pi_P^{mx}}_{\substack{\text{Prinzipal ist} \\ \text{informiert}}} - \underbrace{w_A \pi_P^{mn}}_{\substack{\text{Prinzipal ist nicht informiert,} \\ \text{Agent ist informiert}}} - \frac{dc_P}{dw_P}$$

und

$$\frac{du_A}{dw_A} = \underbrace{\left(1 - w_P\right)\pi_A^{mx}}_{\substack{\text{Prinzipal ist nicht informiert,} \\ \text{Agent ist informiert}}} - \frac{dc_A}{dw_A}.$$

Der Prinzipal erhöht mit w_P die Wahrscheinlichkeit, π_P^{mx} für sich zu garantieren und dabei auf $w_A \pi_P^{mn} < w_A \pi_P^{mx}$ zu verzichten. Der Agent erhöht mit w_A die Wahrscheinlichkeit $(1-w_P)\,\pi_A^{mx}$ zu erhalten. Der Verdrängungseffekt ist nun sichtbar: Je informierter der Prinzipal ist, desto geringer sind die Anreize des Agenten, sich zu informieren. Graphisch gesprochen bedeutet dies, dass die Reaktionskurven des Agenten negativ geneigt sind. Bei Geltung der Monotoniethese wären sie positiv geneigt. Formal zeigt sich die negative Neigung der Reaktionsfunktion des Agenten aufgrund von:

$$\frac{dw_A^R}{dw_P} = -\frac{\dfrac{\partial\left(\left(1 - w_P\right)\pi_A^{mx} - c_A'(w_A)\right)}{\partial w_P}}{\dfrac{\partial\left(\left(1 - w_P\right)\pi_A^{mx} - c_A'(w_A)\right)}{\partial w_A}} = -\frac{\pi_A^{mx}}{c_A''(w_A)} < 0$$

Auch die Reaktionskurve des Prinzipals ist negativ geneigt, wie eine ähnliche Rechnung zeigt. Abbildung 1 skizziert das Gleichgewicht dieses Spiels (den Schnittpunkt der zwei Reaktionskurven), wobei hier die Existenz des Gleichgewichts vorausgesetzt wird.

Der strategische Effekt der Informationserhöhung wird besonders deutlich, wenn man die Informationsentscheidungen sequentiell ablaufen lässt: Der Prinzipal bestimmt als erster seine Informationsanstrengungen und der Agent entscheidet anschließend in Kenntnis der Informationsbemühungen des Prinzipals.

Es kann aufgrund der Informationsverdrängung von Vorteil für den Prinzipal sein, wenn er sich dazu verpflichten kann, relativ wenige Informationen zu sammeln. Denn dann ist der Anreiz des Agenten groß, sich selbst um die Informationen zu kümmern. Umgekehrt: Falls der Chef doch „immer alles selbst" entscheidet, schwinden die Anreize der Mitarbeiter, sich selbst Gedanken zu machen. Um dies positiv auszunutzen, könnte der Prinzipal sich sehr viele Agenten und deren Projekte aufbürden und so die Opportunitätsgrenzkosten der Information für sich erhöhen. Dadurch ergibt sich ein Gleichgewicht mit geringerer eigener Information und erhöhter Information des Agenten, wie dies in Abbildung 2 dargestellt ist.

Abbildung 1: Das Informationsgleichgewicht

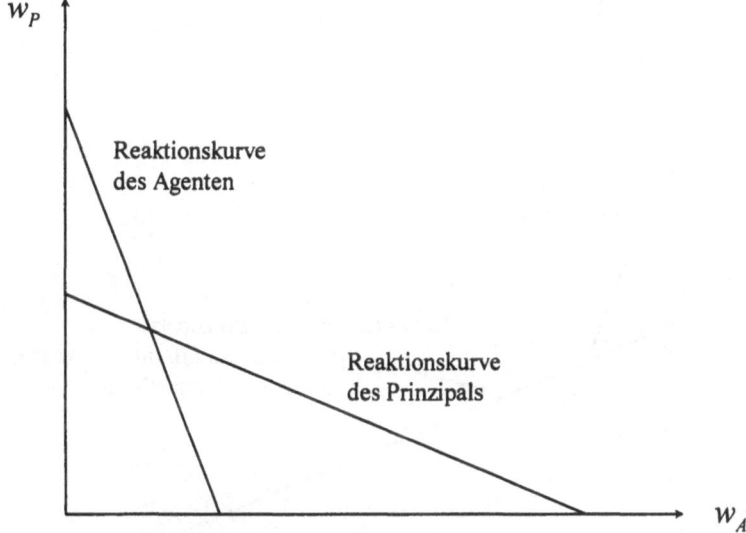

Der Prinzipal hat dann das Maximierungsproblem:

$$\max_{w_P} \quad \underbrace{w_P \pi_P^{mx}}_{\substack{\text{Prinzipal ist} \\ \text{informiert}}} + \underbrace{(1 - w_P) w_A^R (w_P) \pi_P^{mn}}_{\substack{\text{Prinzipal ist nicht informiert,} \\ \text{Agent ist informiert.}}} - c_P(w_P)$$

zu lösen, das zu folgender Bedingung erster Ordnung führt:

$$\underbrace{\pi_P^{mx} - w_A^R(w_P) \pi_P^{mn} - c_P'(w_P)}_{\text{direkter Effekt}} + \underbrace{\frac{dw_A^R}{dw_P}(1 - w_P)\pi_P^{mn}}_{\text{indirekter Effekt}} \overset{!}{=} 0 \; .$$

Aufgrund der Erhöhung der Wahrscheinlichkeit des Prinzipals ergeben sich ein direkter und ein indirekter Effekt. Der direkte Effekt ist bereits oben analysiert worden. Zusätzlich führt jedoch die Erhöhung der Wahrscheinlichkeit der Information auf Seiten des Prinzipals zu einer Verringerung der Informationsbemühung des Agenten, sodass π_P^{mn} mit der Wahrscheinlichkeit $\frac{dw_A^R}{dw_P}(1 - w_P)$ nicht zu bekommen ist. Dies ist der negative indirekte Effekt der Informationsbemühung durch den Prinzipal.

Abbildung 2: Höhere Informationskosten des Prinzipals bewirken höhere Informationsanstrengungen des Agenten

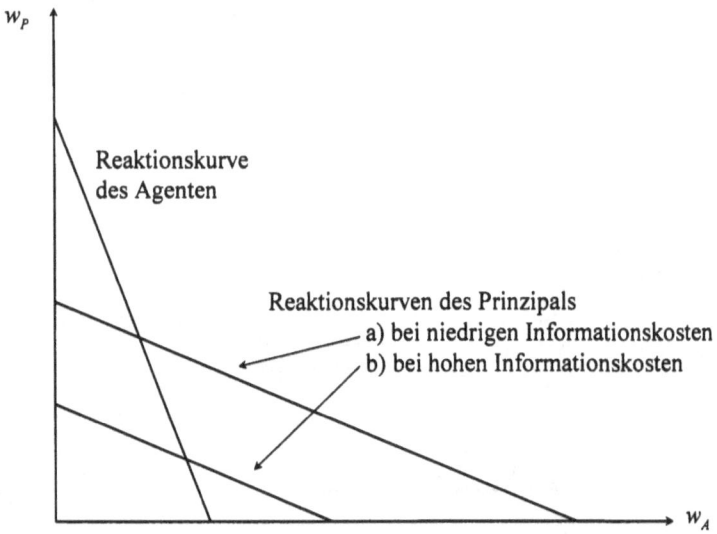

Zusammenfassend ist zu diesem Modell festzuhalten, dass die Monotoniethese – eine Erhöhung der Kontrolle und/oder eine Verstärkung der Anreize führen zur Erhöhung des zielkonformen Verhaltens des Agenten – unter bestimmten Annahmen nicht zu halten ist. Diese Annahmen bestanden in der einfachen Variante darin, dass ein Agent aus drei Projekten mit unterschiedlichen Auszahlungen für beide Vertragsseiten eines vorschlagen kann und der Prinzipal dieses annimmt oder nicht. Welches Projekt vorgeschlagen wird und angenommen bzw. abgelehnt wird, hängt von den beidseitigen Informationsaktivitäten hinsichtlich potentieller Auszahlungen ab. Der Prinzipal ist stark daran interessiert, dass der Agent sich informiert, um einen fundierten Vorschlag zu machen, der besser als der Status quo ist. Der Agent ist aber eher daran interessiert, dass der Prinzipal sich nicht informiert, damit ein auszahlungsgünstigeres Projekt (aus Sicht des Agenten) umgesetzt wird. *Aghion* und *Tirole* (1997) zeigen so die Möglichkeit der Informationsverdrängung endogen im Rahmen eines einfachen Modells, ohne einen Rückgriff auf psychologische Sachverhalte vorzunehmen. In den nächsten Abschnitten soll der vereinfachte Ansatz von *Aghion* und *Tirole* (1997) um zusätzliche Motivatoren extrinsischer und intrinsischer Art erweitert werden, um noch präzisere Aussagen zur Wechselwirkung extrinsischer und intrinsischer Anreize zu treffen. Dazu werden weitere Variablen eingeführt und deren Wirkung auf die Teilnahme- und die Anreizbeschränkung analysiert. Es wird gezeigt, dass die Teilnahmebereitschaft des Agenten, die Qualität seiner Arbeit – hier: die Güte seines Projektvorschlags – und die Informationsanreize eng zusammenhängen.

4. Erweiterungen des Modells von *Aghion* und *Tirole*

4.1. Nutzenmöglichkeitenkurve

Die in Abschnitt 3.2 vorgestellte Modellvariante bzw. das Modell von *Aghion* und *Tirole* (1997) wird nun in vielerlei Richtungen erweitert. Dabei geht es um eine reichhaltigere Modellierung insbesondere extrinsischer Motivationsfaktoren. Lediglich die Delegation wird in dieser Form auch im Originalaufsatz behandelt; die anderen Ergänzungen stammen von den Autoren. Diese Aspekte werden nun der Reihe nach behandelt. Zunächst haben wir jedoch eine Erweiterung des Modells von zwei Projektvorschlägen auf ein Kontinuum zu erläutern. Diese Erweiterung erleichtert die Einführung weiterer Motivationsfaktoren.

Abbildung 3: Auszahlungsmöglichkeiten für Agent und Prinzipal

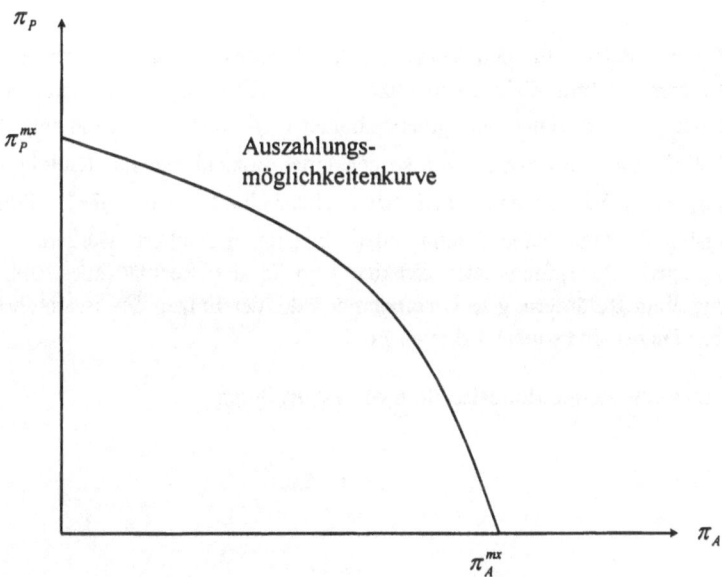

Ein Projektvorschlag des Agenten ist durch die Auszahlung π_A für diesen charakterisiert, wobei $0 \leq \pi_A \leq \pi_A^{mx}$ gelte. Diese Agentenauszahlung π_A ermöglicht eine Auszahlung $\pi_P = \pi_P(\pi_A)$ für den Prinzipal. Wir gehen davon aus, dass der Agent nur *Pareto*-effiziente Vorschläge unterbreitet und dass die Auszahlungsfunktion π_P fallend und konkav ist. Diese Auszahlungskombinationen sind in Abbildung 3 als Auszahlungsmöglichkeitenkurve dargestellt. Neben den Projekten mit Auszahlungskombinationen auf der Auszahlungsmöglichkeitenkurve gibt es ein Projekt „Status quo", das beiden die Auszahlung *0* liefert. Die Menge der Auszahlungskombinationen lautet daher:

$$A := \left\{ \left(\pi_A, \pi_P \right) : 0 \le \pi_A \le \pi_A^{mx}, \pi_P = \pi_P \left(\pi_A \right) \right\} \cup \left\{ (0,0) \right\}.$$

Der Prinzipal und der Agent wissen um die Auszahlung des Status quo, sie wissen ex ante jedoch nicht, wie hoch π_P^{mx} ist. Insbesondere kann der Prinzipal nur dann erkennen, ob der Agent die Interessen des Prinzipals hinreichend berücksichtig hat, wenn der Prinzipal sich ebenfalls informiert hat.

4.2. Vorschlagsbonus

Der Agent macht, falls er informiert ist, einen Vorschlag, der einer Auszahlungskombination auf der Nutzenmöglichkeitenkurve entspricht:

$$\left(\pi_A^v, \pi_P \left(\pi_A^v \right) \right).$$

Der Prinzipal versucht, auf den Vorschlag des Agenten Einfluss zu nehmen. Ist der Prinzipal informiert (mit Wahrscheinlichkeit w_P), weiß er, dass er bestenfalls π_P^{mx} zu erwarten hat. Er legt einen Kongruenzparameter β fest, was bedeutet, dass der Prinzipal $\beta \pi_P^{mx}$ für sich erwartet. Ein so genannter Vorschlagsbonus (Belohnung oder Bestrafung) wird bei Überschreiten bzw. Unterschreiten von $\beta \pi_P^{mx}$ fällig. Der Vorschlagsbonus kann dabei stetig oder unstetig modelliert werden. Unstetige Belohnung bzw. Bestrafung wäre denkbar und in der Realität auch üblich: Die Gewährung einer Beförderung in Unternehmen oder der Entzug des Beamtenstatus im öffentlichen Dienst sind solche diskreten Boni.

Wir setzen eine stetige Bonusfunktion voraus, die durch

$$\frac{\pi_P \left(\pi_A^v \right) - \beta \pi_P^{mx}}{\beta \pi_P^{mx}} s$$

wiedergegeben wird, wobei $s \ge 0$ als Bonusfaktor bezeichnet wird. Abbildung 4 gibt diese Bonusfunktion wieder.

4.3. Delegation und weitere Anreizfaktoren

In der entscheidungsorientierten Betriebswirtschaftslehre besteht das Hauptproblem der Entscheidungsträger (bzw. eines Prinzipals oder einer Instanz) darin, unter Unsicherheit Handlungsalternativen zu generieren und zukünftige Umweltsituationen, deren (subjektive) Eintrittswahrscheinlichkeiten sowie handlungsabhängige Ergebnisse für jeden Umweltzustand abzuschätzen. Aus dieser Konstellation findet eine begründete Alternativenwahl z.B. über das Erwartungswert- bzw. Erwartungsnutzenkonzept statt.

Dabei mag es sich für den Entscheidungsträger lohnen, (Teil-)Entscheidungen zu delegieren. Als Vorteile der Delegation lassen sich die Entlastung der Instanz und die Ausnutzung dezentraler Informationen nennen. Zu viele und zu komplexe Entscheidungssituationen werden für den Prinzipal vereinfacht, indem Teilentscheidungen von Mitarbeitern getroffen werden. Neben diesem Kapazitätseffekt tritt ein weiterer Effekt auf, der in den Erträgen bei alternativer Verwendung der Zeit durch die Instanz besteht. Außerdem kann ein Mitarbeiter mehr bzw. bessere Informationen als der Vorgesetzte haben, deren Transfer mit hohen Informationsübertragungskosten verbunden wäre, oder über höhere Entscheidungsqualitäten und -technologien verfügen, also auf bestimmte (Teil-) Entscheidungen spezialisiert sein.

Abbildung 4: Die lineare Vorschlagsbonusfunktion

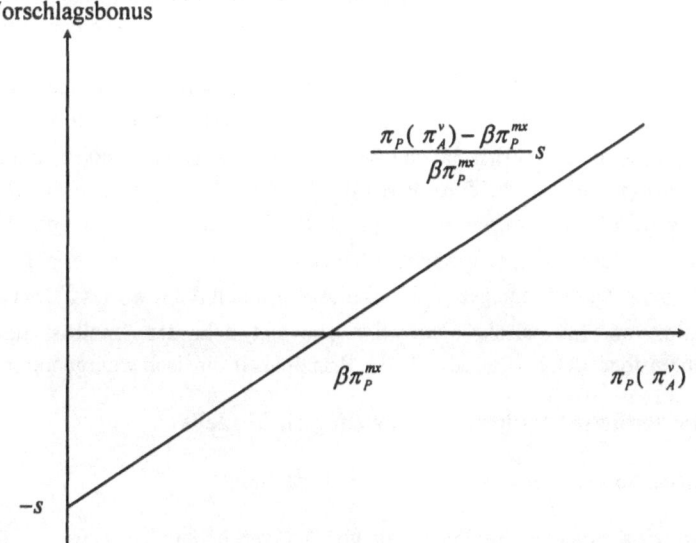

Für die Delegation sind folgende wesentliche Aspekte zu beachten (*Laux* und *Liermann* 1997, S. 170 ff.): Die Kapazität der Beschaffung, Verarbeitung und Übertragung von Informationen, die Verteilung von Informationen, deren Beschaffungsmöglichkeiten und -kosten, die Entscheidungsqualifikation und -güte, Kontrollmöglichkeiten sowie die Ziele der Instanz und der potentiellen Entscheidungsträger. Gerade der letzte Aspekt ist dann von Bedeutung, wenn es um die Motivation der Mitarbeiter geht. Eine Erweiterung des Entscheidungsraumes kann die Mitarbeiter intrinsisch motivieren, wenn auch die Gefahr besteht, dass bei den Mitarbeitern dann Unsicherheit entsteht, wenn sie sich für die Entscheidungen nicht qualifiziert fühlen oder Überlastungseffekte drohen.

Delegation bezieht sich in dem hier gewählten Ansatz auf die Weitergabe der formalen Autorität, also der Entscheidungsgewalt an den Agenten. Formale Autorität kommt üblicherweise Eigentümern oder Vorgesetzten zu. Sie impliziert jedoch keinesfalls reale Autorität, was auf die effektive Kontrolle zurückzuführen ist. Aus Gründen mangelnder Information wird formale Autorität häufig nicht ausgeübt; die reale Autorität kommt dann den mit dem Sachverhalt tatsächlich Befassten zu. Dies wurde bereits in Abschnitt 3.2 modelliert: Sind beide, Prinzipal und Agent, informiert, gilt der Wille des Prinzipals, der die formale Autorität innehat. Ist dagegen nur der Agent informiert, bestimmt dieser das Projekt aufgrund der realen Autorität.

Nun ist denkbar, und dies modellieren *Aghion* und *Tirole* (1997) in sehr überzeugender Weise, dass der Prinzipal auf formale Autorität verzichtet; er delegiert die formale Autorität an den Agenten. Entsprechend unterscheiden *Aghion* und *Tirole* (1997) *P-formale Autorität* (keine Delegation) und *A-formale Autorität* (Delegation). Sind bei Delegation Prinzipal und Agent informiert, wird das Projekt des Agenten durchgeführt.

Unabhängig von der Durchführung des Projektes wird der Vorschlagsbonus bei Überschreiten bzw. Unterschreiten von $\beta \pi_P^{mx}$ fällig (siehe Abschnitt 4.2). Schließlich gibt unser Modell dem Prinzipal die Möglichkeit, bei seiner Entscheidung über das Projekt (falls er die Entscheidung trifft) die Belange des Agenten mehr oder weniger stark zu berücksichtigen. Dies erfolgt mit Hilfe des Anteils, den er von π_P^{mx} für sich reklamiert. Ist der Prinzipal großzügig gegenüber dem Agenten, verlangt er für sich $\gamma\pi_P^{mx}$ mit einem relativ geringen $\gamma < 1$. Der Agent erhält dann $\pi_P^{-1}\left(\gamma\pi_P^{mx}\right) > \pi_P^{-1}\left(\pi_P^{mx}\right) = 0$. Hier sind ex- und intrinsische Motivation gemischt, denn der Anteil ist monetär, wird von Agenten aber u.U. als „goodwill" des Prinzipals intrinsisch wahrgenommen.

4.4. Die zeitliche Struktur des erweiterten Modells

Die zeitliche Abfolge des erweiterten Modells ist diese:

1. Der Prinzipal bindet sich selbst an die von ihm verkündete Vorgabe:

 — Er verkündet, ob er die Entscheidung über das Projekt an den Agenten delegiert oder nicht.

 — Er legt $0 < \beta \le 1$ und $s \ge 0$ fest und damit die Höhe des Vorschlagsbonus als Funktion von π_A^v.

 — Zusätzlich hat er die Wahl klarzustellen, dass er, falls er die Projektauswahl trifft, ein Projekt wählen wird, das ihm selbst $\pi_P^v = \gamma\pi_P^{mx}$ mit $0 \le \gamma \le 1$ einbringt. Verzichtet er hierauf, kann er π_P^v frei wählen.

 — Der Prinzipal legt seine Informationswahrscheinlichkeit fest und wendet dazu die Kosten $c_P(w_P)$ auf.

2. Der Agent trifft seine Informationsentscheidung, die zu den Kosten $c_A(w_A)$ führt.

3. Der Agent schlägt entweder den Status quo vor oder, falls er sich informieren konnte, ein Projekt, das die Auszahlungen $(\pi_A^v, \pi_P(\pi_A^v))$ erbringt.

4. Falls sich der Prinzipal informieren konnte und falls er die formale oder reale Autorität besitzt, implementiert er ein Projekt mit den Auszahlungen $(\pi_P^{-1}(\pi_P^v), \pi_P^v)$. Dabei gilt: $\pi_P^v = \gamma\pi_P^{mx}$. Im Falle der Selbstverpflichtung, einen Teil seiner Auszahlung an den Agenten abzutreten, wird ein Projekt mit $(\pi_P^{-1}(\gamma\pi_P^{mx}), \gamma\pi_P^{mx})$ umgesetzt. Ansonsten bewirkt der Prinzipal die Auszahlungen $(\pi_P^{-1}(\pi_P^{mx}), \pi_P^{mx})$.

Geht man davon aus, dass die Nutzenkomponenten additiv separabel sind, kann man die Nutzenfunktionen von Prinzipal und Agent bei *P-formaler Autorität* so schreiben:

$$(1) \qquad u_P = w_P \underbrace{\left(\pi_P^v - w_A \frac{\pi_P\left(\pi_A^v\right) - \beta\pi_P^{mx}}{\beta\pi_P^{mx}} s \right)}_{\substack{\text{Prinzipal ist} \\ \text{informiert}}} + \underbrace{\left(1 - w_P\right) w_A \pi_P\left(\pi_A^v\right)}_{\substack{\text{Prinzipal ist nicht informiert,} \\ \text{Agent ist informiert}}} - c_P\left(w_P\right)$$

für den Prinzipal und:

$$(2) \qquad u_A = w_P \underbrace{\left(\pi_P^{-1}\left(\pi_P^v\right) + w_A w_e \frac{\pi_P\left(\pi_A^v\right) - \beta\pi_P^{mx}}{\beta\pi_P^{mx}} s \right)}_{\substack{\text{Prinzipal ist} \\ \text{informiert}}} + \underbrace{\left(1 - w_P\right) w_A \pi_A^v}_{\substack{\text{Prinzipal ist nicht informiert,} \\ \text{Agent ist informiert}}} - c_A\left(w_A\right)$$

für den Agenten.

A-formale Autorität führt dagegen zu den Auszahlungen:

$$(3) \qquad u_P = \underbrace{w_A \pi_P\left(\pi_A^v\right)}_{\substack{\text{Agent ist} \\ \text{informiert}}} + w_A w_P \underbrace{\left(-\frac{\pi_P\left(\pi_A^v\right) - \beta\pi_P^{mx}}{\beta\pi_P^{mx}} s \right)}_{\substack{\text{Agent ist informiert,} \\ \text{Prinzipal auch}}} + \underbrace{\left(1 - w_A\right) w_P \pi_P^v}_{\substack{\text{Agent ist nicht informiert,} \\ \text{Prinzipal ist informiert}}} - c_P\left(w_P\right)$$

bzw.:

$$(4) \qquad u_A = \underbrace{w_A \pi_A^v}_{\text{Agent ist informiert}} + \underbrace{w_A w_P \frac{\pi_P\left(\pi_A^v\right) - \beta \pi_P^{mx}}{\beta \pi_P^{mx}} s}_{\substack{\text{Agent ist informiert,} \\ \text{Prinzipal auch}}} + \underbrace{\left(1 - w_A\right) w_P \pi_P^{-1}\left(\pi_P^v\right)}_{\substack{\text{Agent ist nicht informiert,} \\ \text{Prinzipal ist informiert}}} - c_A\left(w_A\right).$$

5. Ergebnisse des erweiterten Modells

In diesem Abschnitt werden die Parameter hinsichtlich ihrer Wirkung auf die Vertragskonstruktion in der Prinzipal-Agent-Beziehung diskutiert. Um sich einer Lösung des Optimierungsproblems des Prinzipals zu nähern, wird das mehrstufige Verfahren beginnend auf der letzten Stufe analysiert.

5.1. Vierte Stufe: Projektauswahl durch den Prinzipal

Das Modell ist so komplex, dass es auch für einfache Spezifikationen der Nutzen-möglichkeitenkurve kaum geschlossen lösbar ist. Dennoch kann man einige interessante und fruchtbare Schlussfolgerungen hinsichtlich der Austauschbeziehungen extrinsischer und intrinsischer Motivation ziehen. Manche ergeben sich direkt aus den Nutzenfunktionen und der zeitlichen Struktur des Modells.

Begonnen wird bei der letzten Stufe des Spiels. Hat sich der Prinzipal nicht auf ein $\gamma < 1$ verpflichtet, wird er auf der letzten Stufe $\pi_P^v = \pi_P^{mx}$ für sich verlangen, das für den Agenten $\pi_P^{-1}\left(\pi_P^{mx}\right) = 0$ ergibt. Ansonsten ergeben sich die Auszahlungen $\gamma \pi_P^{mx}$ für den Prinzipal und $\pi_P^{-1}\left(\gamma \pi_P^{mx}\right)$ für den Agenten.

Wir nehmen zudem an, dass der Prinzipal den Vorschlagsbonus wie versprochen zahlt und auch die einmal getroffene Delegationsentscheidung nicht infrage stellt. Die Begründung für dieses verlässliche Verhalten des Prinzipals mag man darin sehen, dass er nicht nur einem, sondern (immer wieder) mehreren Agenten gegenübersteht. Es liegt im Interesse des Prinzipals, sich als vertrauenswürdig zu erweisen.

5.2. Dritte Stufe: Projektvorschlag des Agenten

Das Optimierungskalkül des Agenten hängt davon ab, ob der Prinzipal die formale Autorität delegiert hat oder nicht. Bei *P-formaler Autorität* erhält man durch Differenzieren von (2) nach π_v^A die Bedingung erster Ordnung:

$$w_P \frac{s}{\beta \pi_P^{mx}} \frac{d\pi_P\left(\pi_A^v\right)}{d\pi_A^v} + \left(1 - w_P\right) \overset{!}{=} 0 \quad \text{oder} \quad \left|\frac{d\pi_P\left(\pi_A^v\right)}{d\pi_A^v}\right| \overset{!}{=} \frac{\left(1 - w_P\right) \beta \pi_P^{mx}}{w_P s}.$$

Erhöht der (informierte) Agent seine Forderung π_v^A um eine Einheit, erhält er diese, falls der Prinzipal nicht informiert ist (d.h. mit Wahrscheinlichkeit $1 - w_P$). Auf der

Negativseite bewirkt eine Erhöhung der Forderung eine Reduzierung des dem Prinzipal Anzubietenden um $\dfrac{d\pi_P\left(\pi_A^v\right)}{d\pi_A^v}$. Ist der Prinzipal informiert und evaluiert er den Vorschlag des Agenten (was mit der Wahrscheinlichkeit w_P passiert), führt die Erhöhung der Forderung dann zu einer Reduzierung des Bonus um $\dfrac{s}{\beta\pi_P^{mx}}\dfrac{d\pi_P\left(\pi_A^v\right)}{d\pi_A^v}$. Aufgrund der Konkavität von π_P ist die Bedingung zweiter Ordnung erfüllt.

Abbildung 5: Höheres Anspruchsniveau und niedrigere Anreize

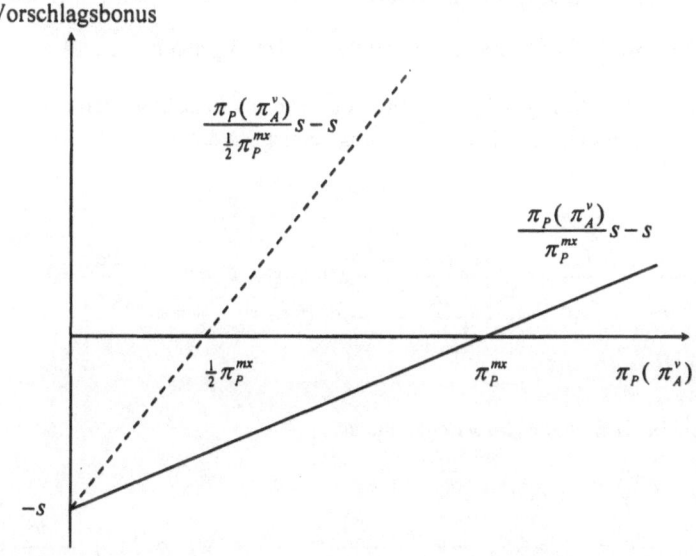

Bei *A-formaler Autorität* (4) wird man dagegen auf die Bedingung erster Ordnung:

$$1+w_P\,\frac{s}{\beta\pi_P^{mx}}\,\frac{d\pi_P\left(\pi_A^v\right)}{d\pi_A^v}\overset{!}{=}0 \quad \text{oder} \quad \left|\frac{d\pi_P\left(\pi_A^v\right)}{d\pi_A^v}\right|\overset{!}{=}\frac{\beta\pi_P^{mx}}{w_P s}$$

geführt.

Aus diesen beiden Bedingungen (π_P ist negativ geneigt und konkav!) lassen sich einige qualitative Aussagen für den Vorschlag des Agenten auf der dritten Stufe treffen:

–   Je informierter der Prinzipal ist, desto niedriger ist die Forderung des Agenten.

– Eine Erhöhung des Bonussatzes, *s*, führt zu einer Verringerung der Forderung des Agenten.

– Der Agent fordert bei *A-formaler Autorität* mehr für sich als bei *P-formaler Autorität*.

– Eine Verringerung des Anspruchniveaus *β* des Prinzipals führt zu einer Verringerung der Forderung des Agenten. Je weniger der Prinzipal haben will, desto mehr bekommt er also! Dieses kontraintuitive Ergebnis wird verständlich, wenn man sich klarmacht, dass es die Steigung der Bonuskurve ist, die für das Verhalten des Agenten verantwortlich ist. In unserem Modell wird die Bonuskurve mit Erhöhung des Anspruchniveaus flacher, die Anreize für den Agenten also geringer. Dies lässt sich auch an Abbildung 5 veranschaulichen.

5.3. Zweite Stufe: Informationsaktivitäten des Agenten

Auf der zweiten Stufe wird der Einfluss der Informationsaktivitäten des Agenten auf seinen Nutzen analysiert. Die Bedingung erster Ordnung lautet bei *P-formaler Autorität*:

$$\frac{du_A}{dw_A} = w_P \underbrace{\frac{\pi_P\left(\pi_A^v\right) - \beta\pi_P^{mx}}{\beta\pi_P^{mx}} s}_{\substack{\text{Prinzipal ist} \\ \text{informiert}}} + \underbrace{\left(1 - w_P\right)\pi_A^v}_{\substack{\text{Prinzipal ist nicht informiert,} \\ \text{Agent ist informiert}}} - \frac{dc_A}{dw_A} \overset{!}{=} 0,$$

während sie bei *A-formale Autorität* so lautet:

$$\frac{du_A}{dw_A} = \underbrace{\pi_A^v}_{\substack{\text{Agent ist informiert}}} + w_P \underbrace{\frac{\pi_P\left(\pi_A^v\right) - \beta\pi_P^{mx}}{\beta\pi_P^{mx}} s}_{\substack{\text{Agent ist informiert} \\ \text{Prinzipal auch}}} - \underbrace{w_P \cdot \pi_P^{-1}\left(\pi_P^v\right)}_{\substack{\text{Agent ist nicht informiert,} \\ \text{Prinzipal ist informiert}}} - \frac{dc_A}{dw_A} \overset{!}{=} 0.$$

Hierbei ist $\pi_P^{-1}\left(\pi_P^v\right) = \pi_P^{-1}\left(\gamma\pi_P^{mx}\right)$ mit:

$$\frac{d\left(\pi_P^{-1}\left(\gamma\pi_P^{mx}\right)\right)}{d\gamma} < 0.$$

Unabhängig von der Verteilung der formalen Autorität gilt, dass bei einer Erhöhung der Informationsaktivitäten des Agenten um eine Einheit:

– der Agent den Bonus $w_P \dfrac{\pi_P\left(\pi_A^v\right) - \beta\pi_P^{mx}}{\beta\pi_P^{mx}} s$ mit größerer Wahrscheinlichkeit erhält und

– die Kosten der Informationssammlung um $\dfrac{dc_A}{dw_A}$ steigen.

Darüber hinaus bewirkt eine Erhöhung der Information um eine kleine Einheit, dass der Agent mit größerer Wahrscheinlichkeit seinen eigenen Vorschlag durchbringt, was ihm $(1 - w_P)\ \pi_A^v$ (bei *P-formaler Autorität*) bzw. π_A^v (bei *A-formaler Autorität*) einbringt.

Bei *A-formaler Autorität* bringt eine Erhöhung von w_A um eine kleine Einheit mit sich, dass der Agent mit größerer Wahrscheinlichkeit $w_P \cdot \pi_P^{-1}\left(\pi_P^v\right)$ nicht erhält. Dies ist um so gravierender, je großzügiger der Prinzipal bei der Wahl von γ war. Wählt der Prinzipal großzügigerweise ein kleines γ, so ist seine Auszahlung $\pi_P^v = \gamma\pi_P^{mx}$ gering und die Auszahlung des Agenten $\pi_P^{-1}\left(\pi_P^v\right)$ hoch. Ein niedriges γ, insbesondere in Verbindung mit einem hohen Informationsstand des Prinzipals, führt somit zu geringen eigenen Informationsbemühungen.

Als Konsequenz ist zu überlegen, wie Delegation der formalen Autorität auf die Anreize zur Informationsbeschaffung wirkt. Dazu betrachten wir für die gegebene Wahrscheinlichkeit w_A und unter Verwendung der Abkürzungen P-f für *P-formal* und A-f für A-formal:

$$\frac{du_A^{A-f}}{dw_A} - \frac{du_A^{P-f}}{dw_A} = w_P\left(\pi_A^v - \pi_P^{-1}\left(\pi_P^v\right)\right).$$

Im Modell von *Aghion* und *Tirole* (1997) ist die Differenz eindeutig positiv; bei *A-formaler Autorität* hat der Agent größeren Anreiz, sich zu informieren als bei *P-formaler Autorität*, denn der Agent wird in diesem Modell immer mehr für sich verlangen, als ihm der Prinzipal anbietet. In unserem Modell muss jedoch $\pi_A^v - \pi_P^{-1}\left(\pi_P^v\right)$ nicht notwendig positiv sein; es mag sich für den Prinzipal lohnen, dem Agenten viel anzubieten, um die Partizipation des Agenten sicher zu stellen, während der Agent für sich eventuell relativ wenig fordert, um in den Genuss des Bonus zu kommen.

Von Wichtigkeit ist nun auch die Abhängigkeit der Information des Agenten von der Information des Prinzipals. Allgemeine Aussagen sind im Gegensatz zum Modell von *Aghion* und *Tirole* (1997) nicht mehr möglich. Dort erhält man das eindeutige Ergebnis negativer Steigung. Dieses Ergebnis wird für $s = 0$ repliziert, falls also keine

Vorschlagsboni vergeben werden und falls die Informationswahrscheinlichkeit den Vorschlag des Agenten nicht beeinflusst $\left(\dfrac{d\pi_A^v}{dw_P} = 0 \right)$.

Nun wird $s > 0$ zugelassen und weiterhin von $\dfrac{d\pi_A^v}{dw_P} = 0$ ausgegangen; dann können die Reaktionskurven positiv geneigt sein, falls die Boni positiv sind und absolut höher als $\pi_P\left(\pi_A^v(w_P)\right)$ bzw. π_P^v. Erhöht der Prinzipal seine Informationswahrscheinlichkeit, hat der Agent den Anreiz, ein Projekt vorschlagen zu können, falls er mit einem positiven Bonus rechnen kann. Siehe dazu Appendix, Abschnitt 1.

5.4. Erste Stufe: Beeinflussung der Teilnahme- und Anreizbeschränkungen durch den Prinzipal

5.4.1. Parameter zur Beeinflussung der Teilnahme- und Anreizbeschränkungen

Der Prinzipal verfügt auf der ersten Stufe über fünf Parameter der Beeinflussung: Er entscheidet über die Zuordnung der formalen Autorität auf sich selbst oder auf den Agenten (Delegation), er legt das Anspruchsniveau β und den Vorschlagsbonussatz s fest und er verpflichtet sich auf γ. Wir nehmen an, dass auch die Informationswahrscheinlichkeit w_P des Prinzipals auf der ersten Stufe festgelegt wird. Diese Parameter werden der Reihe nach diskutiert und dabei die jeweilige Möglichkeit für die Lockerung der Teilnahmebeschränkung und der Anreizbeschränkung untersucht.

Die Anreizbeschränkungen beziehen sich dabei zum einen auf die Informationsanstrengungen des Agenten (w_A), zum anderen auf die Güte des Projektvorschlages aus der Sicht des Prinzipals $\left(\pi_P(\pi_A^v)\right)$. Untersucht wird nun, welche Aktionsparameter des Prinzipals tendenziell dazu geeignet sind, die Teilnahme des Agenten (T), ein hohes Informationsbemühen bzw. das Zeigen von Initiative (I) und einen guten Projektvorschlag (V) hervorzubringen. Als Kürzel werden die Symbole T^+, I^+ und V^+ verwendet, um anzudeuten, dass der Aktionsparameter die Agenten tendenziell zur Teilnahme, zum Zeigen von Initiative und zum Vorschlagen eines für den Prinzipal vorteilhaften Projektes bewegen. Analog werden T^-, I^- und V^- verwendet, wenn die Aktionsparameter negative Wirkung auf die Teilnahme, die Initiative und die Güte des Projektvorschlages haben.

5.4.2. Informationsaktivitäten des Prinzipals zu den Projekten

Der Prinzipal informiert sich über die Projekte, über die er eventuell einen Projektvorschlag erhalten wird. Die Informationswahrscheinlichkeit w_P ist ein recht zentraler Parameter für den Prinzipal. Er wirkt auf die Informationswahrscheinlichkeit des Agenten und auf den Vorschlag des Agenten ein. Entsprechend werden zwei Arten von strategischen Effekten identifiziert: Die *I-strategischen Effekte* wirken über die

Veränderung von w_A und die *V-strategischen Effekte* über die Veränderung des Vorschlages des Agenten. Zur Abschätzung der komplizierten Wirkungskette sind entsprechend die Grenznutzen für den Prinzipal bei *P-formaler Autorität* und *A-formaler Autorität* zu formulieren. Siehe dazu Appendix, Abschnitt 2.1.

Bei *P-formaler Autorität* bewirkt eine Erhöhung der Information um eine kleine Einheit direkte und indirekte Effekte. Zu den direkten Effekten zählen:

– ein Trade off-Effekt: der Prinzipal erhält π_P^v, verzichtet jedoch auf $w_A \pi_P\left(\pi_A^v\right)$;

– der Prinzipal muss den erwarteten Vorschlagsbonus $w_A \dfrac{\pi_P\left(\pi_A^v\right)-\beta\pi_P^{mx}}{\beta\pi_P^{mx}}s$ auszahlen

   (er kann auch negativ sein); und

– die Kosten der Informationssammlung steigen.

Erhöht der Prinzipal seine Informationswahrscheinlichkeit, so reduziert der Agent im allgemeinen seine Informationsbemühungen (siehe jedoch Abschnitt 5.3). Dies hat Einfluss auf die Auszahlung des Prinzipals:

– der Bonus $w_P \dfrac{\pi_P\left(\pi_A^v\right)-\beta\pi_P^{mx}}{\beta\pi_P^{mx}}s$ muss nun mit geringerer Wahrscheinlichkeit

   ausgezahlt werden; und

– der Prinzipal erhält, soweit er selbst nicht informiert ist, $\pi_P\left(\pi_A^v\right)$ mit geringerer Wahrscheinlichkeit.

Die Erhöhung der Informationswahrscheinlichkeit w_P beeinflusst die Forderung π_A^v des Agenten negativ, wie in Abschnitt 5.2 festgestellt wurde. Daher muss ein Prinzipal, der seine Informationswahrscheinlichkeit erhöht, bedenken, dass

– die Höhe des vom Prinzipal zu zahlenden Vorschlagsbonus um $\dfrac{d\pi_P}{d\pi_A^v}\dfrac{d\pi_A^v}{dw_P}w_A\dfrac{w_P s}{\beta\pi_P^{mx}}$

   ansteigt; und

– die Forderung des Agenten sinkt und damit, soweit der Prinzipal im Gegensatz zum Agenten nicht selbst informiert ist, $\dfrac{d\pi_P}{d\pi_A^v}\dfrac{d\pi_A^v}{dw_P}$ für den Prinzipal zusätzlich anfällt.

Man kann nun die Effekte bei *A-formaler Autorität* in ähnlicher Weise durchspielen. Die Unterschiede der Effekte rühren von der unterschiedlich verteilten formalen Autorität her. Beispielsweise erhält der Prinzipal bei *A-formaler Autorität* π_P^v nur mit der Wahrscheinlichkeit $1-w_A$.

Die Informationserhöhung des Prinzipals wirkt aber auch auf die Erfüllung der Teilnahmebeschränkung. Eine eindeutige Richtung ist nicht anzugeben. Entsprechend der *P-formalen* und der *A-formalen Autorität* ergeben sich unterschiedliche Auswirkungen von w_P auf die Nutzenfunktionen des Agenten. Siehe dazu Appendix, Abschnitt 2.2.

Außerdem wirken die Aktionsparameter des Prinzipals zusammen. Bei *P-formaler Autorität* ist der Agent eventuell nicht sehr erfreut über eine gute Informationslage des Prinzipals, wenn er selbst sehr gut informiert ist: Ist der Prinzipal informiert, setzt er ein Projekt mit der Auszahlung $\pi_P^{-1}(\pi_P^v)$ für den Agenten durch. Ist der Prinzipal nicht informiert, erhält der Agent π_A^v. Bei *A-formaler Autorität* kann der Agent eher von der Information durch den Prinzipal profitieren; diese wird nur dann für die Projektauswahl verwandt, wenn der Agent nicht informiert ist.

Je großzügiger der Prinzipal bei seiner Entscheidung über das Projekt ist (d.h. je niedriger γ ist), desto eher ist dem Agenten daran gelegen, dass der Prinzipal sich auch selbst gut informiert. Muss der Agent Input für den Informationsprozess des Prinzipal leisten (dies wurde hier nicht modelliert), ist von daher ein niedriges γ anzuraten.

5.4.3. Entscheidung des Prinzipals über die Allokation der Autorität

Ein wesentlicher Parameter des Modells ist die Allokation der Autorität. Man erhält die Differenz:

$$u_P^{P-f} - u_P^{A-f} = w_A w_P \left(\pi_P^v - \pi_P(\pi_A^v) \right),$$

wobei die Auswirkungen der Delegation auf die Informationsbemühungen und auf die Forderung des Agenten unterdrückt werden. Offenbar sind die direkten Effekte der Delegation negativ, falls der Prinzipal für sich selbst mehr fordert, als ihm der Agent anbietet. Zudem bietet der Agent dem Prinzipal bei Delegation ein „schlechteres" Projekt an. Allerdings erhöht die Delegation typischerweise die Informationsbemühung des Agenten, was dem Prinzipal häufig angenehm ist.

Um die direkten Auswirkungen der Delegation auf den Agenten zu bestimmen, berechnen wir, wiederum unter Auslassung der indirekten Effekte, die Differenz:

$$u_A^{A-f} - u_A^{P-f} = w_A w_P \left(\pi_A^v - \pi_P^{-1}(\pi_P^v) \right).$$

Durch Delegation kann der Prinzipal die Teilnahmebeschränkung lockern, denn Delegation ermöglicht dem Agenten bei beidseitiger Information, den eigenen Vorschlag anstelle des Vorschlages des Prinzipals zu realisieren.

Die Frage der Delegation ist natürlich nicht unabhängig von den Informationsbemü-hungen zu sehen. Dazu wird für gegebene Wahrscheinlichkeit w_P:

$$\frac{du_P^{P-f}}{dw_P} - \frac{du_P^{A-f}}{dw_P} = w_A \left(\pi_P^v - \pi_P \left(\pi_A^v (w_P) \right) - \frac{d\pi_P}{d\pi_A^v} \frac{d\pi_A^v}{dw_P} w_P \right)$$

betrachtet, wobei die Auswirkungen der Delegation auf die Forderung des Agenten unterdrückt werden.

Im Modell von *Aghion* und *Tirole* (1997) ist die Differenz eindeutig positiv; bei *P-formaler Autorität* ist der Prinzipal also begieriger als bei *A-formaler Autorität*, Informationen über die Projekte zu erhalten. Denn der Prinzipal wird in diesem Modell immer mehr für sich verlangen, als ihm der Agent anbietet, und der indirekte Effekt, der über den Einfluss auf die Forderung des Agenten läuft, ist nicht existent. Im vorliegen-den erweiterten Modell muss jedoch zum einen $\pi_P^v - \pi_P \left(\pi_A^v (w_P) \right)$ nicht notwendig positiv sein; eventuell bietet der Agent dem Prinzipal viel an, um in den Genuss des Bonus zu kommen, und der Prinzipal hat sich eventuell auf ein relativ geringes γ verpflichtet. Zum anderen ist der strategische Effekt $\dfrac{d\pi_P}{d\pi_A^v} \dfrac{d\pi_A^v}{dw_P}$ positiv, sodass auch von daher der Prinzipal möglicherweise bei *P-formaler Autorität* weniger Informationen sammelt als bei *A-formaler Autorität*. Gerade bei Delegation ist der Prinzipal darauf angewiesen, dass der Agent ihm einen guten Vorschlag unterbreitet. Der Agent ist jedoch eher bereit, dem Prinzipal viel anzubieten, falls er sich kontrolliert fühlt.

Damit kann Delegation die Teilnahmebeschränkung lockern (T^+), wenn beide gut informiert sind. Hinsichtlich der Anreizbeschränkungen ergibt sich in der Regel eine Lockerung für die Informationsbemühungen des Agenten (I^+), jedoch nicht für die Güte des Vorschlags (V^-). Diese kann der Prinzipal durch eigene Informationsbemü-hungen jedoch verbessern.

5.4.4. Höhe des Vorschlagsbonus

Durch Festlegung des Anspruchsniveaus β und des Bonussatzes s bestimmt der Prinzipal die Höhe des Vorschlagsbonus. Im linearen Fall wurde dieser Bonus spezifiziert als:

$$\frac{\pi_P \left(\pi_A^v \right) - \beta \pi_P^{mx}}{\beta \pi_P^{mx}} s .$$

Er wird jedoch nur gezahlt, wenn der Agent sich informieren konnte (sonst kann er gar keinen Vorschlag machen) und wenn der Prinzipal sich informieren konnte (sonst kennt er π_P^{mx} nicht). Ex ante wird der Vorschlagsbonus mit einer Wahrscheinlichkeit von $w_A w_P$ fällig.

In Abschnitt 5.2 wurde festgestellt, dass bezüglich der Güte des Projektvorschlages s monoton und β (etwas erstaunlich) nicht monoton wirkt (V^+). Erwartet der Agent einen positiven Bonus (also $\pi_P(\pi_A^v) > \beta \pi_P^{mx}$), werden seine Anreize zur Informationsbeschaffung mit s steigen und mit β sinken. Damit sind die Informationsbeschaffungsanreize gegenläufig (also: I^+, I^-). Die Teilnahmebeschränkung ist (bei erwartetem positivem Vorschlagsbonus) ebenfalls mit relativ hohem s und relativ geringem β zu lockern (T^+). Der Bonus wirkt als extrinsische Motivation.

5.4.5. Verpflichtung des Prinzipals auf γ

Verpflichtet sich der Prinzipal nicht auf ein $\gamma < 1$, wird er auf der letzten Stufe $\pi_P^v = \pi_P^{mx}$ für sich verlangen, was $\gamma = 1$ bedeutet. Welche Gründe gibt es nun für den Prinzipal, sich auf weniger zu verpflichten? Aus Partizipationsgründen mag der Prinzipal die Wünsche des Agenten berücksichtigen wollen und $\pi_P^{-1}(\pi_P^v)$ großzügig wählen. Zu prüfen ist, welche Konsequenzen dies für die Anreize des Agenten hat.

Anreize auf die Güte des Vorschlags, den der Agent unterbreitet, gibt es gar nicht. Bei *A-formaler Autorität* führt ein niedriges γ, insbesondere in Verbindung mit einem hohen Informationsstand des Prinzipals, jedoch zu geringeren Informationsbemühungen des Agenten (I^-). Denn bei *A-formaler Autorität* möchte der Agent seinem großzügigen Prinzipal gerne die Entscheidung überlassen.

6. Zusammenfassung und Ausblick

In diesem abschließenden Kapitel wollen wir noch einmal zusammenfassen, wie die einzelnen Parameter in unserem Modell auf die Teilnahme- und Anreizbeschränkungen wirken. Dabei wird sowohl auf die Partizipationsbedingung als auch auf die Anreize zur Informationsbeschaffung und zur Güte der vorgeschlagenen Projekte Bezug genommen werden.

Zentrale Fragen sind, ob sich aus Sicht des Prinzipals die Delegation von Entscheidungen an den Agenten, hier: die formale Autorität, lohnt und wie mögliche Anreizparameter auf die Lösung wirken. Dazu war ein mehrstufiger Lösungsprozess des Optimierungsproblems zu analysieren. Die erste Stufe war jedoch nur zu lösen, wenn die Konsequenzen der folgenden Stufen berücksichtigt wurden. Die Lösung erfolgte beginnend auf der letzten Stufe.

Auf der vierten Entscheidungsstufe ist die Höhe der Auszahlungen davon bestimmt, ob der Prinzipal sich auf eine Selbstverpflichtung ($\gamma < 1$) festgelegt hat. Auf der vorletzten Entscheidungsstufe, auf der der Agent einen Vorschlag unterbreitet, ist bereits deutlich geworden, dass eine Mischung von ex- und intrinsischer Motivation nicht völlig beliebig vorgenommen werden kann. So verringert sich die Forderung des Agenten aufgrund eines niedrigeren Anspruchsniveaus des Prinzipals und aufgrund verstärkter Kontrollen. Das Wechselspiel von Anreiz und Kontrolle ist somit in diesem Modell gut zu verdeutlichen.

Hinsichtlich der Informationsaktivitäten des Agenten auf der zweiten Stufe stellt man eine Wechselwirkung mit den Informationsaktivitäten des Prinzipals fest. Über die Modellergebnisse bei *Aghion* und *Tirole* (1997) hinaus ist festzustellen, dass hohe und positive Boni den Agenten veranlassen können, auf eine Informationserhöhung des Prinzipals seinerseits mit einer vermehrten Anstrengung zu reagieren.

Der Prinzipal beachtet auf der ersten Stufe - Gestaltungsüberlegungen hinsichtlich Anreiz- und Partizipationsbeschränkungen - fünf Parameter der Beeinflussung: Es wird über die Delegation formaler Autorität an den Agenten entschieden. Außerdem sind das Anspruchsniveau β und der Vorschlagsbonussatz s festzulegen. Gegebenenfalls entscheidet sich der Prinzipal für eine konkrete Selbstverpflichtung (γ) und legt sich auch auf eine Informationswahrscheinlichkeit w_P fest.

Das erweiterte Modell führt u.a. zu folgenden Ergebnissen. Delegation kann die Teilnahmebeschränkung lockern (T^+). Für die Anreizbeschränkungen ergibt sich eine Verbesserung für die Initiative um Information des Agenten (I^+), aber nicht für die Qualität des Vorschlags (V^-). Allerdings wird der Agent dem Prinzipal mehr anbieten, falls dieser gut informiert ist.

Die Güte des Projektvorschlages wird durch den Vorschlagsbonus s monoton und das Anspruchsniveau β (etwas erstaunlich) nicht monoton beeinflusst. Wenn der Agent von einem positiven Bonus ausgeht, werden seine Anreize zur Informationsbeschaffung mit s steigen und mit β sinken. Die Informationsbeschaffungsanreize sind also gegenläufig (I^+, I^-). Die Teilnahmebeschränkung ist (bei erwartetem positivem Vorschlagsbonus) ebenfalls mit relativ hohem s und relativ geringem β zu lockern (T^+). Der Bonus wirkt hier als extrinsische Motivation.

Delegation führt - wie bereits erwähnt - zu höheren Informationsanstrengungen (w_A) des Agenten (I^+). *P-formale Autorität* wirkt der Motivation entgegen. Dann gilt auch, dass mit steigendem Anspruchsniveau des Prinzipals ein Agent sich weniger informieren wird. Ein hohes Anspruchsniveau führt bei dem Agenten unabhängig von der Allokation der Autorität demotivierend. Die Erträge der Informationsbemühungen sinken nämlich, wenn die Aussichten auf einen entsprechenden Anteil geringer werden (I^-).

Schließlich konnten wir das Ergebnis begründen, dass ein großzügiger Prinzipal (mit einem niedrigen γ) zwar die Teilnahmebeschränkung lockert. Eine unerwünschte Wirkung besteht jedoch darin, dass der Agent in seinen Informationsbemühungen nachlässt (I^-).

Ausgehend von den Beiträgen von *Aghion* und *Tirole* behandelte dieser Beitrag extrinsische und intrinsische Motivatoren. Wir konnten zeigen, dass der Ansatz von *Aghion* und *Tirole* geeignet ist, die Verdrängungshypothese von *Frey*, die dieser mit intrinsischer Motivation eher postuliert als begründet, aufgrund von extrinsischen Motivatoren zu bestätigen. In einer Weiterentwicklung wurden im Beitrag weitere Motivatoren in einem Modell vereinigt. Der Zweck dieser Zusammenführung bestand darin, die Wirkungszusammenhänge zwischen verschiedenen Anreizmechanismen aufzuzeigen. Dabei konnten wir trotz des recht allgemein gehaltenen Modells einige interessante qualitative Aussagen treffen.

Zwar ist das hier vorgestellte Modell recht komplex. Dennoch kann man sich weitere Faktoren vorstellen und modellieren, die das Entscheidungsverhalten von Prinzipal und Agent in der Realität beeinflussen:

−   Zunächst könnte der Prinzipal einen Informationsbonus „ausloben". Diese Vergütung wird bei Unterbreiten eines Vorschlags gezahlt; es ist hierfür nicht notwendig, dass der Prinzipal die Güte des Vorschlags beurteilen kann. Einen Informationsbonus zu zahlen, kann jedoch mit Problemen behaftet sein. Dieser Bonus könnte den Agenten dazu verführen, eine große Anzahl von nur sehr wenig unterschiedlichen Projekten jeweils als neues Projekt anzubieten (Aktionismus).

−   Sodann wird in der verhaltenswissenschaftlich orientierten Literatur stark betont, dass der Agent eventuell „Gestaltungsfreude" hat. In der Terminologie von *Frey* (1997, S. 431) würde man die intrinsische Motivation durch die "interessante Aufgabe" erreichen. Der Agent hat einen Nutzen davon, dass das von ihm recherchierte Projekt umgesetzt wird. Bei gegebenen Informationswahrscheinlichkeiten führt Delegation eher als *P-formale Autorität* zur Realisierung von Gestaltungsfreude.

−   Des Weiteren mag man annehmen, dass der Agent Nutzen daraus zieht, formale Autorität zu besitzen. Motivierend wirkt - wie auch in der verhaltenswissenschaftlichen Literatur vertreten wird - der Statuszuwachs aus der formalen Autorität. Allerdings ist auch Demotivation denkbar, wenn nämlich der Agent sich mit der Aufgabe überfordert fühlt.

−   Schließlich könnte man annehmen, dass der Agent nicht gerne detailliert kontrolliert wird. Auch hier ist die umgekehrte Annahme denkbar: Der Agent hat dann einen Nutzen davon, dass der Prinzipal Interesse an seiner Arbeit zeigt.

Natürlich kann ein theoretisches Modell keine Rezepte für die Personalwirtschaft liefern. Der Zweck eines solchen Modells besteht dagegen darin, wichtige Anregungen für die Gestaltung von Anreizsystemen in der Personalpolitik abzuleiten.

Appendix

1. Die Steigung der Reaktionskurve des Agenten

Die Steigung der Reaktionskurve des Agenten ist bei *P-formaler Autorität* aufgrund des Theorems über die implizite Funktion:

$$\frac{dw_A^R}{dw_P} = -\frac{\partial\left(\frac{du_A^{P-f}}{dw_A}\right)}{\partial w_P} = -\frac{\frac{\pi_P\left(\pi_A^v\right)-\beta\pi_P^{mx}}{\beta\pi_P^{mx}}s+w_P\frac{\frac{d\pi_P}{d\pi_A^v}\frac{d\pi_A^v}{dw_P}}{\beta\pi_P^{mx}}s-\pi_A^v+\left(1-w_P\right)\frac{d\pi_A^v}{dw_P}}{-c_A''(w_A)}$$

und bei *A-formaler Autorität*:

$$\frac{dw_A^R}{dw_P} = -\frac{\partial\left(\frac{du_A^{P-f}}{dw_A}\right)}{\partial w_P} = -\frac{\left(1-w_P\right)\frac{d\pi_A^v}{dw_P}+\frac{\pi_P\left(\pi_A^v\right)-\beta\pi_P^{mx}}{\beta\pi_P^{mx}}s+w_P\left(\frac{d\pi_A^v}{dw_P}+\frac{\frac{d\pi_P}{d\pi_A^v}\frac{d\pi_A^v}{dw_P}}{\beta\pi_P^{mx}}s\right)-\pi_P^{-1}\left(\pi_A^v\right)}{-c_A''(w_A)}.$$

Falls die Forderung des Agenten nicht durch w_P beeinflusst wird und falls $s = 0$ ist, ergeben sich bei *P-formaler Autorität*:

$$\frac{dw_A^R}{dw_P} = -\frac{\partial\left(\frac{du_A^{P-f}}{dw_A}\right)}{\partial w_P} = -\frac{\pi_A^v}{c_A''(w_A)}$$

und bei *A-formaler Autorität*:

$$\frac{dw_A^R}{dw_P} = -\frac{\partial\left(\frac{du_A^{A-f}}{dw_A}\right)}{\partial w_P}\Bigg/\frac{\partial\left(\frac{du_A^{A-f}}{dw_A}\right)}{\partial w_A} = -\frac{\pi_P^{-1}\left(\pi_P^v\right)}{c_A''(w_A)}.$$

Die von *Aghion* und *Tirole* ermittelte negative Steigung ergibt sich hier auch. Lässt man nun $s > 0$ zu und geht weiterhin von $\dfrac{d\pi_A^v}{dw_P}$ aus; dann erhält man bei *P-formaler Autorität*:

$$\frac{dw_A^R}{dw_P} = -\frac{\partial\left(\frac{du_A^{P-f}}{dw_A}\right)}{\partial w_P}\Bigg/\frac{\partial\left(\frac{du_A^{P-f}}{dw_A}\right)}{\partial w_A} = -\frac{-\dfrac{\pi_P\left(\pi_A^v\right)-\beta\pi_P^{mx}}{\beta\pi_P^{mx}}s+\pi_A^v}{c_A''(w_A)}$$

und bei *A-formaler Autorität*:

$$\frac{dw_A^R}{dw_P} = -\frac{\partial\left(\frac{du_A^{A-f}}{dw_A}\right)}{\partial w_P}\Bigg/\frac{\partial\left(\frac{du_A^{A-f}}{dw_A}\right)}{\partial w_A} = -\frac{-\dfrac{\pi_P\left(\pi_A^v\right)-\beta\pi_P^{mx}}{\beta\pi_P^{mx}}s+\pi_P^{-1}\left(\pi_P^v\right)}{c_A''(w_A)}.$$

Nun können die Reaktionskurven positiv geneigt sein, falls die Boni positiv sind und absolut höher als $\pi_P\left(\pi_A^v(w_P)\right)$ bzw. π_P^v.

2. Erste Stufe: Beeinflussung der Teilnahme und Anreizbeschränkungen

2.1. Informationsaktivitäten des Prinzipals

Grenznutzen des Prinzipals bei *P-formaler Autorität*:

$$\frac{du_P}{dw_P} = \underbrace{\pi_P^v}_{\substack{\text{direkter Effekt:}\\\text{Auszahlung von }\pi_P^v}} - \underbrace{w_A \pi_P\left(\pi_A^v\right)}_{\substack{\text{direkter Effekt:}\\\text{Nichterhalt von }\pi_P\left(\pi_A^v\right)\\\geq 0}} - w_A \underbrace{\frac{\pi_P\left(\pi_A^v\right) - \beta\pi_P^{mx}}{\beta\pi_P^{mx}}s}_{\substack{\text{direkter Effekt:}\\\text{Auszahlung des Bonus}}} - \underbrace{\frac{dc_P}{dw_P}}_{\substack{\text{direkter Effekt:}\\\text{Kosten der Information}}}$$

$$- w_P \underbrace{\frac{\pi_P\left(\pi_A^v\right) - \beta\pi_P^{mx}}{\beta\pi_P^{mx}}s\frac{dw_A}{dw_P}}_{\substack{\text{1.I-strategischer Effekt:}\\\text{Auszahlung des Bonus}}} + \underbrace{\frac{dw_A}{dw_P}\pi_P\left(\pi_A^v\right)\left(1 - w_P\right)}_{\substack{\text{2.I-strategischer Effekt:}\\\text{Nichterhalt von }\pi_P\left(\pi_A^v\right)}}$$

$$- \underbrace{\frac{d\pi_P}{d\pi_A^v}\frac{d\pi_A^v}{dw_P}w_A\frac{w_P s}{\beta\pi_P^{mx}}}_{\substack{\text{1.V-strategischer Effekt:}\\\text{Höhe des Bonus}}} + \underbrace{\frac{d\pi_P}{d\pi_A^v}\frac{d\pi_A^v}{dw_P}w_A\left(1 - w_P\right)}_{\substack{\text{2.V-strategischer Effekt:}\\\text{Beeinflussung der Forderung}}}$$

Grenznutzen des Prinzipals bei *A-formaler Autorität*:

$$\frac{du_P}{dw_P} = \underbrace{\left(1 - w_A\right)\pi_P^v}_{\substack{\text{direkter Effekt:}\\\text{Auszahlung von }\pi_P^v}} - w_A \underbrace{\frac{\pi_P\left(\pi_A^v\right) - \beta\pi_P^{mx}}{\beta\pi_P^{mx}}s}_{\substack{\text{direkter Effekt:}\\\text{Auszahlung des Bonus}}} - \underbrace{\frac{dc_P}{dw_P}}_{\substack{\text{direkter Effekt:}\\\text{Kosten der Information}}}$$

$$- w_P \underbrace{\frac{\pi_P\left(\pi_A^v\right) - \beta\pi_P^{mx}}{\beta\pi_P^{mx}}s\frac{dw_A}{dw_P}}_{\substack{\text{1.I-strategischer Effekt:}\\\text{Auszahlung des Bonus}}} + \underbrace{\frac{dw_A}{dw_P}\pi_P\left(\pi_A^v\right)}_{\substack{\text{2.I-strategischer Effekt:}\\\text{Nichterhalt von }\pi_P\left(\pi_A^v\right)}} - \underbrace{\frac{dw_A}{dw_P}w_P\pi_P^v}_{\substack{\text{3.I-strategischer Effekt:}\\\text{Auszahlung von }\pi_P^v}}$$

$$- \underbrace{\frac{d\pi_P}{d\pi_A^v}\frac{d\pi_A^v}{dw_P}w_A\frac{w_P s}{\beta\pi_P^{mx}}}_{\substack{\text{1.V-strategischer Effekt:}\\\text{Höhe des Bonus}}} + \underbrace{\frac{d\pi_P}{d\pi_A^v}\frac{d\pi_A^v}{dw_P}w_A}_{\substack{\text{2.V-strategischer Effekt:}\\\text{Beeinflussung der Forderung}}}$$

2.2 Auswirkungen der Informationserhöhung des Prinzipals auf die Teilnahmebeschränkung

Die Auswirkungen von w_P auf die Nutzenfunktion des Agenten bei P-*formaler Autorität* unter Vernachlässigung der strategischen Effekte:

$$\frac{du_A}{dw_P} = \underbrace{\pi_P^{-1}\left(\pi_P^v\right) + w_A\frac{\pi_P\left(\pi_A^v\right) - \beta\pi_P^{mx}}{\beta\pi_P^{mx}}s}_{\substack{\text{Prinzipal ist}\\\text{informiert}}}$$

$$- \underbrace{w_A\pi_A^v}_{\substack{\text{Prinzipal ist nicht informiert,}\\\text{Agent ist informiert}}}$$

und bei *A-formaler Autorität*:

$$\frac{du_A}{dw_P} = w_A \underbrace{\frac{\pi_P\left(\pi_A^v\right) - \beta\pi_P^{mx}}{\beta\pi_P^{mx}} s}_{\substack{\text{Agent ist informiert,} \\ \text{Prinzipal auch}}} + \underbrace{\left(1 - w_A\right) \cdot \pi_P^{-1}\left(\pi_P^v\right)}_{\substack{\text{Agent ist nicht informiert,} \\ \text{Prinzipal ist informiert}}}.$$

Literatur

Aghion, Philippe und *Jean Tirole* (1997), Formal and Real Authority in Organizations, in: Journal of Political Economy, Vol. 105, S. 1-29.

Alderfer, Clayton P. (1972), Existence, Relatedness, and Growth: Human Needs in Organizational Settings, New York.

Argyris, Chris (1990), Overcoming Organizational Defenses, Boston.

Bénabou, Roland und *Jean Tirole* (2003), Intrinsic and Extrinsic Motivation, in: Review of Economic Studies, Vol. 70, S. 489-520.

Deci, Edward L. und *Richard M. Ryan* (1985), Intrinsic Motivation and Self-Determination in Human Behavior, New York.

Fehr, Ernst und *Armin Falk* (2002), Psychological Foundations of Incentives. in: European Economic Review, Vol. 46, S. 687-724.

Fehr, Ernst und *Klaus M. Schmidt* (1999), A Theory of Fairness, Competition and Cooperation, in: Quarterly Journal of Economics, Vol. 114, No. 3, S. 817-868.

Frey, Bruno S. (1993a), Motivation as a Limit to Pricing, in: Journal of Economic Psychology, Vol. 14, S. 635-664.

Frey, Bruno S. (1993b), Shirking or Work Morale? The Impact of Regulating, in: European Economic Review, Vol. 37, S. 1523-1532.

Frey, Bruno S. (1997), On the relationship between intrinsic and extrinsic work motivation, in: International Journal of Industrial Organization, Vol. 15, S. 427-439.

Frey, Bruno S. und *Reto Jegen* (2001), Motivation Crowding Theory, in: Journal of Economic Surveys, Vol. 15, No. 5, S. 589-611.

Frey, Bruno S. und *Margit Osterloh* (1997), Sanktionen oder Seelenmassage? Motivationale Grundlagen der Unternehmensführung, in: Die Betriebswirtschaft, Jg. 57, S. 307-321.

Herzberg, Frederick (1966), Work and the Nature of Man, Cleveland.

Kunz, Alexis H. und *Dieter Pfaff* (2002), Agency Theory, Performance Evaluation, and the Hypothetical Construct of Intrinsic Motivation, in: Accounting, Organizations and Society, Vol. 27, S. 275-295.

Laux, H. und *F. Liermann* (1997), Grundlagen der Organisation, 4. Aufl., Berlin.

Murdock, Kevin (2002), Intrinsic Motivation and Optimal Incentive Contracts, in: RAND Journal of Economics, Vol. 33, No. 4, S. 650-671.

Porter, Lyman W. und *Edward E. III Lawler* (1968), Managerial Attitudes and Performance, New York.

Rabin, Matthew (2002), A Perspective on Psychology and Economics, in: European Economic Review, Vol. 46, S. 657-685.

Rosenstiel, Lutz v. (1993), Motivation von Mitarbeitern, in: *Rosenstiel, Lutz v.; E. Regnet* und *M. Domsch* (Hrsg.), Führung von Mitarbeitern, Stuttgart, S. 155-172.

Schanz, Günther (1991), Motivationale Grundlagen der Gestaltung von Anreizsystemen, in: *Schanz, Günther* (Hrsg.), Handbuch Anreizsysteme in Wirtschaft und Verwaltung, Stuttgart, S. 3-50.

Tirole, Jean (2002), Rational Irrationality: Some Economics of Self-management, in: European Economic Review, Vol. 46, S. 633-655.

Vroom, Victor H. (1964), Work and Motivation, New York.

Weinert, Ansfried B. (1998), Organisationspsychologie, 4. Aufl., Weinheim.

Autoren und Seminarteilnehmer

Altenburg, Prof. Dr. Ursula, Universität Leipzig

Berger, Dipl.-Vw. Pablo, Universität Leipzig

Bültel, PD Dr. Dirk, Universität Leipzig

Casajus, Dr. André, Universität Leipzig

Decker, Dipl.-Hdl. Carolin, Universität Leipzig

Diedrich, Prof. Dr. Ralf, Universität Leipzig

Dietrich, Dr. Diemo, Inst. f. Wirtschaftsforschung, Halle.

Emons, Prof. Dr. Winand, Universität Bern

Ewert, Prof. Dr. Ralf, Universität Frankfurt/Main

Eymann, Dr. Torsten, Universität Freiberg

Falk, Prof. Dr.Armin, Universität Bonn

Föhr, Prof. Dr. Silvia, Universität Leipzig

Folk, Matthias, Universität Leipzig

Frey, Prof. Dr. Rüdiger, Universität Leipzig

Giersberg, Miriam, Universität Leipzig

Goldammer, Prof. Dr. Gerd, Universität Leipzig

Hasse, Prof. Dr. Rolf, Universität Leipzig

Hauck, Dipl.-Vw. Achim, Universität Leipzig

Jenkis, Prof. Dr. Helmut, Hannover

Kaiser, Dipl.-Vw Karolina, Universität Leipzig

Köhler, Dipl.Km. Anja, Universität Leipzig

Köpping, Dipl.-Vw. Heide, Universität Leipzig

Legutke, Dipl.-Vw. Tobias, Universität Leipzig

Lenk, Prof. Dr. Thomas, Universität Leipzig

Lutsyk, Dipl.-Oec. Tetyana, Universität Leipzig

Marin, Prof. Dr. Dalia, Universität München

Mikoleizik, Dipl.-Vw.sozw.R. Andreas, Universität Leipzig

Quaas, PD Dr. Friedrun, Universität Leipzig

Quaas, Dr. Georg, Universität Leipzig

Rauch, M.A. Mathias, Universität Leipzig

Rautenberg, Prof. Dr. Hans Günter, Universität Leipzig

Röder, Dr. Wilfried, Universität Leipzig

Rohde, Dipl.-Oec. Claudia, Universität Leipzig

Teichertova, Dipl.-Math. Jana, Universität Leipzig

Thiele, Dipl. Wirt.-Ing. Sandra, Universität Leipzig

Tröger, Dipl.-Vw. Lothar, Universität Leipzig

Vollmer, Prof. Dr. Uwe, Universität Leipzig

Wiese, Prof. Dr. Harald, Universität Leipzig

Zeitfracht Medien GmbH
Ferdinand-Jühlke-Straße 7
99095 Erfurt, Deutschland
produktsicherheit@kolibri360.de